Praise for *College*

"To renew higher education in an age of secular pluralism, Delbanco summons his colleagues to a defense of the university's role in fostering humane and democratic impulses.... Delbanco's agenda for reform—curricular, pedagogical, financial, and technological—will stimulate a much-needed national dialogue."
—Bryce Christensen, *Booklist*

"Delbanco explores American higher education in a manner befitting a scholar of Melville and the Puritans, with a humanist's belief in lessons from history and in asking what the right thing is to do.... College has always been a microcosm of society, so a book about it is also about how we're doing as a country."
—Clare Malone, *American Prospect*

"A thoughtful and insightful look at American college's exceptionalism and pit-falls.... Whether you're in college, thinking about college or just paying for it, it's a good read to help better understand one of America's oldest and finest insti-tutions. And if we want it to stay that way, we all better get schooled about it."
—Kacie Flynn, *Vox Magazine, Missourian*

"The 'Was' part is an illuminating reminder of the Puritan origin of early colleges, such as Harvard and Princeton, where only wealthy males needed apply and where religion, literature and philosophy dominated the curricula. The 'Is' sec-tion considers the prohibitive cost, the woefully underprepared applicants, the self-centered teachers and the dominance of research over instruction of under-graduates at today's colleges. Obviously the 'Should Be' is Delbanco's motive in this effort.... He dreams of the day when college teachers are back in the class-rooms, working collaboratively to bring their youngsters into this new century."
—Kathleen Daley, *Newark Star Ledger*

"A thoughtful, literate, and gracefully written reminder of what higher education needs to be."
—Elizabeth R. Hayford, *Library Journal*

"Refreshingly, Delbanco's examination of what college was doesn't turn into a longing backward look.... This book is a result of what Delbanco says is two decades of visiting more than 100 colleges of all types, from community colleges to the undergraduate divisions of research universities. It is also the product of extensive reading: He seems to have digested every self-flagellating and self-congratulating essay, every cri de coeur and jeremiad about higher ed that has been produced since scholars sat down together in collegium."
—Sebastian Stockman, *Kansas City Star*

"This is a brief, well-researched book, and an insightful account of the factors that shape the current higher educational landscape."
—Dennis O'Brien, *Commonweal*

"An eloquent book—a combination of jeremiad, elegy and call to arms."
—Alan Cate, *Cleveland Plain Dealer*

"In *College*, [Delbanco] looks to the lengthy and dynamic history of higher education in America as a lens through which to examine its current crises and unsettled future."
—Serena Golden, *Inside Higher Ed*

"'Every year the teacher gets older while the students stay the same age.' This has always been true, but Delbanco's observation has a poignant weight today when college is always justified as being for something, whether for the economy, or for democracy, or for social mobility, and not as a place that exists as a community asking questions together, trying to unify knowledge to make sense of our lives—in short, as a place where we pursue the truth."

—Angus Kennedy, *Spiked Review of Books*

"At a time when many are trying to reduce the college years to a training period for economic competition, Delbanco reminds readers of the ideal of democratic education. . . . The American college is too important 'to be permitted to give up on its own ideals,' Delbanco writes. He has underscored these ideals by tracing their history. Like a great teacher, he has inspired us to try to live up to them."

—Michael S. Roth, *New York Times Book Review*

"Andrew Delbanco does a marvelous job tracing the evolution of one of the most treasured institutions in the United States, 'college,' in terms of the ideal of such an institution and the challenges it is facing. . . . Delbanco's book would be a great one for students and scholars in the fields of educational philosophy, history of education, educational policy, and other related fields. It would also be a good read for anyone who is interested in the development of higher education in the United States."

—Shouping Hu, *Teachers College Record*

"What commends [this] book is its richness of reference and its willingness to charge colleges and universities with lapses that should sow insomnia among administrators."

—James Morris, *Wilson Quarterly*

"*College: What It Was, Is, and Should Be* gives a clear picture of all the forces, both within and outside the university, working against the liberal arts."

—Joseph Epstein, *Weekly Standard*

"Andrew Delbanco's recent book is to be praised, for it reminds us that college should be about character formation and not a surrender to a customer service mentality that inflates accomplishments to please future employers, placate doting parents and repair fragile egos. . . . Enlightening."

—Robert J. Parmach, *America* magazine

"Delbanco ought to be required reading for all involved in higher education."

—*Richmond Times-Dispatch*

"A small book that deserves to be widely read. . . . At the book's center is a deep commitment to what the liberal arts, at their best, can do for students, and a passionate plea that, in our rush to solve real and perceived educational challenges of many kinds, we not neglect the liberal arts, but rather determine to extend their benefits to as many students as possible."

—Robert Wiltenberg, *Continuing Higher Education Review*

ANDREW DELBANCO

COLLEGE

What It Was, Is, and Should Be

With a new preface by the author

PRINCETON UNIVERSITY PRESS

Princeton and Oxford

Copyright © 2012 by Princeton University Press

Published by Princeton University Press, 41 William Street,
Princeton, New Jersey 08540

In the United Kingdom: Princeton University Press, 6 Oxford Street,
Woodstock, Oxfordshire OX20 1TW

press.princeton.edu

Seventh printing, and first paperback printing, with a new preface by the author, 2013
Paperback ISBN 978-0-691-15829-7

The Library of Congress has cataloged the cloth edition of this book as follows

Delbanco, Andrew, 1952–
College : what it was, is, and should be / Andrew Delbanco.
      p.   cm.
Includes bibliographical references and index.
ISBN 978-0-691-13073-6 (alk. paper)
1. Education, Higher—Aims and objectives—United States. I. Title.
LA227.4.D455 2012
378.73–dc23   2011039399

British Library Cataloging-in-Publication Data is available

This book has been composed in Garamond Premier Pro and Trajan Pro

Printed on acid-free paper. ∞

Printed in the United States of America

10 9 8 7

The true college will ever have one goal—not
to earn meat, but to know the end and aim
of that life which meat nourishes.

—W.E.B. DuBois

To my students

CONTENTS

PREFACE to the Paperback Edition

Since the first edition of this book appeared a little less than a year ago, public demand that our colleges scrutinize, justify, and reform themselves has grown from a murmur to a roar. Cries for change are coming from every direction—from families struggling to pay tuition, from students contending with debt, from employers seeking competent graduates, and from politicians insisting on accountability.

They all have good reasons. College in America costs too much and students learn too little. Moreover, in the past few months a flood of headlines has further inflamed public doubt about the state of higher education. The University of Virginia was rocked by a confrontation between its board and its president over its ability to adapt to the future; appalling details about sexual abuse at Penn State continued to come out; the president of Florida A&M resigned under fire after a student died from the effects of a brutal hazing; a cheating scandal erupted at Harvard; a committee of the United States Senate issued a blistering report on the unscrupulous practices of some for-profit colleges. These are just a few of the events that have stoked public anger at the discrepancy between the cost of college and its value—an anger of which I got a personal taste in the form of several emails accusing me of shilling for colleges on behalf of student-loan racketeers.

Beneath this emotion is a stratum of truth. The gap between resources and needs in America's colleges has never been wider. Everywhere we see unsustainable costs: deferred maintenance on overbuilt campuses where space is wasted (remember Monday morning and Friday afternoon classes?); science labs in continual need of updating; athletic facilities that must, by the tyrannical laws of status and rivalry, be bigger and better than those of the competition; the ballooning cost of financial aid for less affluent students—all in the face of relentless growth in tuition as well as precipitous decline in public subsidies.

One response to the seemingly infinite pressure on finite funds has been to look to the new digital technologies for salvation. MIT and Harvard (later joined by Berkeley, the University of Texas, Georgetown, and Wellesley College) have announced an online partnership (edX) in order to spread knowledge— and, not incidentally, their brand names—all over the world, while the number of students enrolled in Coursera, a collaboration of some thirty universities, including Stanford, Princeton, and Penn, now is approaching 2 million. Since this book first appeared, the acronym MOOC (Massive Open Online Courses) has become part of the language. Meanwhile, young entrepreneurs are raising significant capital for a growing list of for-profit ventures, including, among many others, Straighterline, which offers low-cost online courses with credits transferable to partner institutions; Inigral, an online "private, branded community" meant to supplement or replace the "networking" that's said to be among the benefits of college; and Minerva, an online "elite" university that promises top-quality education at a much lower price than the Ivies.

Given this rapid pace of change, the president of Stanford foresees a "tsunami" bearing down on us that threatens to sweep away the features of the traditional college that are the subject of this book: classrooms where teachers and students meet face to face; degrees awarded upon completion of a certain number of local credits; campuses with dorms, gyms, labs; and so on. Serious people believe that all this will soon be a vestige of the past in some cases, to be replaced by a virtual world where professors accustomed to speaking to a few hundred students will reach a few hundred thousand via the web. In other cases, "blended," or "hybrid," teaching, combining in-person with online, will become the new norm.

Some of these alarms and opportunities will doubtless prove false or illusory, as is always the case with warnings and promises about the future. But it's foolish to doubt that higher education is on the verge of upheaval. While we wait to see how well digital instruction will work for students, and how much money it will actually save or earn, one thing seems certain: traditional colleges will have to do more with less. That means concentrating on their core mission, which, in turn, means that they must have a clear sense of what, in fact, that mission has been. This book is my effort to answer that question.

The burden of my argument is that the American college has long been devoted to three central principles. The first, deeply ingrained in our culture, is that people should not be constrained by the circumstances of their birth, but should have the chance to discover their passions and pursue them as far as their talents allow. Second, the college classroom has been a rehearsal space for democracy—a place where students learn to speak and listen with civility to peers whose perspective on the world differs from their own. And finally, the American college has always been about more than the transmission of information or the inculcation of skills; it has been, at its best, about helping young people prepare for lives of meaning and purpose. To the extent that we compromise these principles, we imperil our democracy, which surely faces perils enough. At a time when the call for innovation has never been louder, the biggest innovation we could make is to retrieve these fundamental values and renew our commitment to them.

What has heartened and touched me is how many people inside and outside academia remain passionately devoted to these principles. When this book first came out, I heard from faculty at institutions where budgets are low and skepticism runs high about the worth of liberal education, who wrote to say that the book helped them make the case to their deans and provosts for the importance of what they do. I heard in the same vein from deans, provosts, and presidents—a reminder that our colleges are filled at all levels with people of deep commitment and constancy to their students. And I heard from students. I have had the pleasure and privilege of speaking at several institutions to gatherings of first-year students newly arrived on campus and looking forward, with hope and anxiety, to their college years. Their excitement at the prospect of venturing beyond themselves has confirmed, in ways that delighted me, that the highest educational ideals remain alive for those to whom they matter most.

I have also heard from graduates who look back upon their college years with satisfaction and gratitude. Here, reproduced with permission, is one email that captures well the practical value of the putatively impractical education this book seeks to defend:

> I graduated from Aquinas College, a private liberal arts
> school, with a BA in History in 2010. The culture sur-
> rounding a history degree graduate does not leave much
> optimism for employment opportunities. . . . I was lucky
> however and got my foot in the door for a position as
> Managing Director at a raceway because I knew the right
> people. Going into the position blind was truly terrify-
> ing. I would be responsible for all aspects of running
> a business: management, accounting, PR, marketing,
> human resources, etc. What were the secret tools and
> methods that those Business majors picked up? How
> could I cope without them?
>
> I don't know what I missed out on in those business
> courses, but I can tell you that it is not essential. The truly
> important skills are learned in the liberal arts: global think-
> ing, problem solving, communication, goal setting, and
> most importantly the ability to learn that which I did not
> yet understand. Using my foundations in the humanities
> I have created an atmosphere of pride and respect that has
> caused a 70% increase in revenues in just a single year.
>
> Tell your students fear not.

These comments speak to a point often missed in discussions of higher education: that the choice between vocational and liberal studies is a false one. Students in programs focused on specific job skills such as computer programming, engineering, or nurs-ing need—and deserve—to have their minds stretched by the big questions raised by history, science, philosophy, and the arts. By the same token, students in traditional liberal arts fields need to gain the concrete skills that are required in a demanding labor market. This is not a question of either/or.

Ultimately, as the dedication attests, I wrote this book for students. As several reviewers have pointed out, it proposes no large-scale solutions for the endemic problems now facing higher education. What it does propose is that our colleges will continue to serve our society well only if they advance into the future equipped with an understanding of the past. To that end, the pages that follow may be read as the biography of an endangered institution.

December 2012

PREFACE

When colleagues heard that I was writing a book about college, they would sometimes ask me why. It seemed to me a surprising question, like asking a doctor why she is interested in hospitals and patients, or an architect why he cares about buildings and the people who live or work in them. It is true that most books on this subject are written by scholars who study it as a professional specialty, or by retired presidents who have led one kind of academic institution or another. So why would a professor of American literature distract himself with it? Occasionally, the question even carried a hint of suspicion or disapproval, as if I were losing interest in my "field."

I have two answers, which seem worth stating here at the outset of the book that I ended up writing. The first can be stated very briefly. Undergraduate education—how its purposes and practices have been expressed and enacted—is a fascinating part of America's history. I hope this book will convey some sense of that fascination.

The second answer is a little more extended, and requires a story. Soon after I arrived at Columbia University twenty-six years ago, a meeting of the college faculty was called to discuss the latest budget crisis. (There is always a crisis—but this one was especially severe.) At that meeting, the president of the university announced that the deficit in the budget of the arts and sciences division, of which the undergraduate college is a main part, was growing so rapidly that he had no choice but to urge an end to Columbia's policy of "need-blind admissions" in order to rein in expenditures on financial aid. As a new arrival, I was unfamiliar with most of my new colleagues, but I recognized a number of distinguished faculty in the room. One by one, they rose in protest. They said that the president's proposal would not stand. They said that the policy of need-blind admissions expressed a basic value: that our college must be open to any qualified applicant regardless of financial means. A motion was made, and passed by acclamation, that the faculty would give back a percentage of its scheduled salary raise to be paid into the pool of funds reserved for financial aid. The president retreated, and the need-blind admissions policy was retained.

Of course, I voted yes. Like Ishmael in *Moby-Dick*, "I was one of that crew; my shouts had gone up with the rest; my oath had been welded with theirs." And, like Ishmael vowing to join the hunt for the white whale, I had no idea of what I was saying. On my way across campus after the meeting, I confessed to myself that need-blind admissions, though it sounded like justice and fairness and goodness itself, was for me just a slogan. I had no grasp of what it meant. Where did the idea come from? Who decides who needs what? What does the policy cost? How is it paid for?

I don't think my ignorance was unusual. Faculty often know next to nothing about how the institutions in which they work became what they are, how they are organized, where the lines of authority begin and end, or just about anything else outside their home department or division. In some ways, this disconnectedness is a good thing. It allows the freedom to concentrate on whatever subject stirs the passion and made academic work exciting in the first place. But in other ways it is a problem, because it hinders faculty from participating in the life of their college or university as informed citizens.

In the years following that meeting, I undertook to educate myself about American higher education so I could better understand certain central questions—not just about admissions and financial aid, but about curriculum, teaching techniques, the financial structure of academic institutions, and, more generally, the premises and purposes of college education. In so doing, I followed the principle that governs my own teaching—that in order to comprehend problems of the present, it is helpful to know something about the past. After a while, I organized a colloquium for graduate students—future faculty—to discuss the history, current state, and prospects for colleges and universities in the United States. With my colleague Roger Lehecka, former Columbia College dean of students, I also began to teach a course for undergraduates about equity and access in American higher education. Eventually, when I felt I had become reasonably informed about these issues, I began to write about them. This book is the result.

I hope it will be a useful book not only for present and future college faculty, but for present and future college students as well. And at a time when Americans are bombarded with soundbites and half-truths about our colleges and universities—about their high cost, low student achievement, (putatively) pampered faculty, and so on—I also have had a broader audience in mind. It's my hope that anyone concerned with what it means, and what it takes, to educate citizens in our republic will find some interest here too.

New York City

September 2011

COLLEGE

INTRODUCTION

Imagine a list of American innovations that would convey some sense of our nation's distinctiveness in the world. Depending on the list-maker's mood, it might include the atom bomb, jazz, the constitutional rights of criminal defendants, abstract expressionism, baseball, the thirty-year fixed rate mortgage, and fast food. Everyone would have a different version; but unless it included the American college, it would be glaringly incomplete.

At least in a vague way, we all know this. Americans, particularly those in or aspiring to the middle class, talk about college all the time—from the toddler's first standardized test, through the nail-biting day when the good or bad news arrives from the admissions office, to the "yellow, bald, toothless meetings in memory of red cheeks, black hair, and departed health," as Ralph Waldo Emerson described his twentieth college reunion nearly two centuries ago (men aged more quickly in those days). The best week of the year for your local news vendor is probably the week *U.S. News & World Report* comes out with its annual college rankings issue. Rival publications from *Playboy* to *Princeton Review* peddle their own lists of best party colleges, best "green" colleges, best for minorities, best for cost versus value, and, of course, their versions of the best of the best. If you Google the word "college"—even if you screen out such irrelevancies as "electoral college" or "college of cardinals"—you run the risk of overloading your computer. When I tried it not long ago, I got 52,800,000 hits.

Most of the chatter does little, however, to answer the question of what a good college is or ought to be. In fact, the criteria we use to assess the quality of a college—number of publications by its faculty, size of endowment, selectivity in admissions, rate of alumni giving, even graduation rates—tell very little about what it does for its students. In a *New Yorker* article not long ago, Malcolm Gladwell pointed out that faculty compensation, which is one standard measure of college quality, may actually have an inverse relation to faculty engagement in teaching—since the best-paid professors are likely to be at research universities, where undergraduate teaching tends to be a sideline activity.[1]

Yet we use the terms "college" and "university" interchangeably. "She went to Michigan," we say, or "he goes to Oberlin"— not bothering with the noun that follows the name, as if a college and a university were the same thing. They are not. They are, to be sure, interconnected (most college teachers nowadays hold an advanced university degree), and a college may exist as a division or "school" within a university. But a college and a university have—or should have—different purposes. The former is about transmitting knowledge of and from the past to undergraduate students so they may draw upon it as a living resource in the future. The latter is mainly an array of research activities conducted by faculty and graduate students with the aim of creating new knowledge in order to supersede the past.

Both of these are worthy aims, and sometimes they converge, as when a college student works with a scholar or scientist doing "cutting-edge" or "groundbreaking" research—terms of praise that would have been incomprehensible before the advent of the modern university. More often, however, these purposes come into competition if not conflict, especially as one moves up the ladder of prestige. As the man who created one of the world's great universities, the University of California, acknowledged with unusual honesty, "a superior faculty results in an inferior concern for undergraduate teaching." It has been nearly fifty years since Clark Kerr identified this "cruel paradox" as "one of our more pressing problems." Today it is more pressing than ever.[2]

But what, exactly, is at stake in college, and why should it matter how much or little goes on there? At its core, a college should be a place where young people find help for navigating the territory between adolescence and adulthood. It should provide guidance, but not coercion, for students trying to cross that treacherous terrain on their way toward self-knowledge. It should help them develop certain qualities of mind and heart requisite for reflective citizenship. Here is my own attempt at reducing these qualities to a list, in no particular order of priority, since they are inseparable from one another:

1. A skeptical discontent with the present, informed by a sense of the past.
2. The ability to make connections among seemingly disparate phenomena.
3. Appreciation of the natural world, enhanced by knowledge of science and the arts.
4. A willingness to imagine experience from perspectives other than one's own.
5. A sense of ethical responsibility.

These habits of thought and feeling are hard to attain and harder to sustain. They cannot be derived from exclusive study of the humanities, the natural sciences, or the social sciences, and they cannot be fully developed solely by academic study, no matter how well "distributed" or "rounded." It is absurd to imagine them as commodities to be purchased by and delivered to student consumers. Ultimately they make themselves known not in grades or examinations but in the way we live our lives.

Still, encouraging and fostering them should be among the aims of a college education, and in the pages that follow I will have critical things to say about how well we are doing at meeting this responsibility. I have been reluctant, however, to join the hue and cry that the condition of our colleges is dire. Everywhere, and all the time—or so, at least, it seems—we hear about "administrative bloat, overpriced tuition, overpaid teachers, decadent facilities, and subpar educational experiences."[3] This cry of crisis is very old. As early as 1776, Abigail Adams was writing to her husband that college students "complain that their professor . . . is taken off by public business to their great detriment," and that education has "never been in a worse state." More than a century later, the president of Stanford University declared that "the most pressing problem in American higher education is the care of underclassmen, the freshmen and sophomores."[4] It would not be difficult to compile a list of similar laments stretching from the colonial period into the present.

So anyone who writes about the state of our colleges today has a boy-who-cried-wolf problem. But that does not mean that the wolf is not at the door. The American college is going through a period of wrenching change, buffeted by forces—globalization; economic instability; the ongoing revolution in information technology; the increasingly evident inadequacy of K–12 education; the elongation of adolescence; the breakdown of faculty tenure as an academic norm; and, perhaps most important, the collapse of consensus about what students should know—that make its task more difficult and contentious than ever before. For now, let me pause on just one of these forces—what is sometimes called the "casualization" or "adjunctification" of the faculty—by way of the CEO of a high-tech company who offers an ominous analogy.

Once upon a time, he says, thousands of pianists provided live music in America's movie theaters; then, one day, the technology of the soundtrack arrived, and suddenly all those musicians went out of business except for "two piano players [who] moved to L.A." to produce recorded movie music. By analogy, course "content" (readings, lectures, problem sets, quizzes, and the like) can now be uploaded onto interactive websites, and instructors hired, essentially as pieceworkers, to evaluate students' work online. People who, in the pre-digital past, would have been teachers in college classrooms will have to "go and do more productive things"—just as those obsolete piano players had to do.[5]

It is no accident that science-oriented institutions such as MIT and Carnegie Mellon are leading the way in developing new technologies for "online" learning; and while, as former Princeton president William Bowen puts it, these technologies have already proven their value for fields "where there is a 'single right answer' to many questions" (Bowen's example is statistics), the jury is out on whether they can be successfully adapted as a means to advance genuinely humanistic education. As the British education scholar Alison Wolf writes, "we have not found any low-cost, high-technology alternatives to expert human teachers"—at least not yet.[6]

This specter, though it is spreading across the landscape of higher education, will be only a shadow edging into view on the periphery of the story to be told in this book. That is because my focus is on the so-called elite colleges, which have so far been relatively immune to the gutting of the faculty that is already far advanced at more vulnerable institutions. Yet the role of faculty is changing everywhere, and no college is impervious to the larger forces that, depending on one's point of view, promise to transform, or threaten to undermine, it. As these forces bear down upon us, neither lamentation nor celebration will do. Instead, they seem to me to compel us to confront some basic questions about the purposes and possibilities of a college education at a time when there is more and more demand for it and less and less agreement about what it should be. In the face of these uncertainties, this book is an attempt to state some fundamental principles that have been inherited from the past, are under radical challenge in the present, and, in my view, remain indispensable for the future.

Before the story begins, I should say a bit more about my choice of emphasis. As one scholar puts it, over the history of American higher education, "the pattern set by Harvard, Yale, and Princeton . . . became that of colleges all over the country."[7] Along with a handful of others, these institutions have established curricular norms, admissions procedures, financial aid principles, and even the rites and ceremonies of college life. However unhealthy the public obsession with them may be, or how disproportionate the attention they command (a gross disproportion considering their relatively small enrollments), it remains the case that it is these institutions through which the long arc of educational history can best be discerned. And if they have peculiar salience for understanding the past, they wield considerable influence in the present debate over which educational principles should be sustained, adapted, or abandoned in the future.

But if my institutional focus is relatively narrow, I have also tried to keep in view the enormous diversity, as one writer puts it, of the "widely varying instances of what we call college."[8] One of the great strengths of America's educational "system" is that it has never really been a system at all. There are roughly four thousand colleges in the United States: rural, urban, and suburban; non-profit, for-profit; secular, religious; some small and independent, others within large research institutions; some highly selective, others that admit almost anyone who applies and has the means to pay. Over the last twenty years or so, I have visited more than a hundred colleges of many kinds, which has helped, I hope, to mitigate the risk of imagining them as close variations of the ones I know best.

Even a quick scan of this landscape reveals how radically the meaning of college is changing, and how rapidly the disparities among institutions are growing.[9] For a relatively few students, college remains the sort of place that Anthony Kronman, former dean of Yale Law School, recalls from his days at Williams, where his favorite class took place at the home of a philosophy professor whose two golden retrievers slept on either side of the fireplace "like bookends beside the hearth" while the sunset lit the Berkshire hills "in scarlet and gold." For many more students, college means the anxious pursuit of marketable skills in overcrowded, underresourced institutions, where little attention is paid to that elusive entity sometimes called the "whole person." For still others, it means traveling by night to a fluorescent office building or to a "virtual classroom" that exists only in cyberspace. It is a pipe dream to imagine that every student can have the sort of experience that our richest colleges, at their best, provide. But it is a nightmare society that affords the chance to learn and grow only to the wealthy, brilliant, or lucky few. Many remarkable teachers in America's community colleges, unsung private colleges, and underfunded public colleges live this truth every day, working to keep the ideal of democratic education alive.

And so it is my unabashed aim in this book to articulate what a college—any college—should seek to do for its students. A short statement of that obligation can be found in John Updike's last novel, *Terrorist*, about the son of an absentee Egyptian immigrant father and an Irish American mother growing up in Rust Belt New Jersey. The boy is persuaded by a local imam that he should learn the pieties and purities of his father's faith rather than expose himself to moral corruption in an American college. For different reasons, the boy's mother also sees no need for her son to extend his student days beyond high school. When the college counselor disagrees and tries to change her mind, she asks, "What would he study at college?" The counselor replies, "What anybody studies—science, art, history. The story of mankind, of civilization. How we got here, what now?"

In the pages that follow, these two questions will be asked about college itself: "How we got here, what now?"

ONE

WHAT IS COLLEGE FOR?

One of the peculiarities of the teaching life is that every year the teacher gets older while the students stay the same age. Each fall when classes resume, I am reminded of the ancient Greek story of a kindly old couple who invite two strangers into their modest home for a meal. No matter how much the hosts drink, by some mysterious trick their goblets remain full even though no one pours more wine. Eventually, the guests reveal themselves as gods who have performed a little miracle to express their thanks. So it goes in college: every fall the teacher has aged by a year, but the class is replenished with students who stay forever young.[1]

For this and many other reasons, the relation between teacher and student is a delicate one, perhaps not as fraught as that between parent and child, or between spouses or siblings, but sometimes as decisive. Henry James captured it beautifully in a story called "The Pupil," which is not about a college teacher but about a private tutor who has come to love the child whom he is trying to save from his parents:

When he tried to figure to himself the morning twilight
of childhood, so as to deal with it safely, he perceived that
it was never fixed, never arrested, that ignorance, at the
instant one touched it, was already flushing faintly into
knowledge, that there was nothing that at a given moment you could say a clever child didn't know. It seemed
to him that he both knew too much to imagine [the
child's] simplicity and too little to disembroil his tangle.

Embedded in this passage is the romantic idea that the student
possesses latent knowledge of ultimate things, and that the
teacher's task is to probe for the lever that releases knowledge
into consciousness.

In trying to make it happen, even—perhaps especially—a
good teacher can sometimes seem brutal. The famously demanding Joseph Schwab, for example, who taught for years in the "Bio-
logical Sequence" course at the University of Chicago, was known
for "putting one student in the hot seat for a while . . . working
that person as thoroughly and creatively as possible before moving on to another." One Chicago alumnus, Lee Shulman, former
president of the Carnegie Foundation for the Advancement of
Teaching, recalls that sitting in Schwab's class "fostered clammy
hands, damp foreheads" and, to put it mildly, "an ever-attentive
demeanor."[2] This figure of the "tough love" teacher—think of
Annie Sullivan in *The Miracle Worker* or Professor Kingsfield in
The Paper Chase—has become a cliché of our culture, and like all
clichés, it contains some truth, though doubtless simplified and
unduly generalized. It also seems less and less pertinent to the
present. At most colleges today, a student experiencing such anxiety would likely drop the class for fear of a poor grade (compulsory courses of the sort that Schwab taught have become rare),

and the teacher would risk a poor score on the end-of-semester evaluations.[3]

Whatever the style or technique, teaching at its best can be a generative act, one of the ways by which human beings try to cheat death—by giving witness to the next generation so that what we have learned in our own lives won't die with us. Consider what today we would call the original "mission statement" of America's oldest college. The first fund-raising appeal in our history, it was a frank request by the founders of Harvard for financial help from fellow Puritans who had stayed home in England rather than make the journey to New England. Despite their mercenary purpose, the words are still moving almost four hundred years after they were written:

> After God had carried us safe to New England, and we had
> built our houses, provided necessaries for our livelihood,
> reared convenient places for God's worship, and settled
> the civil government, one of the next things we longed for
> and looked after was to advance learning and perpetuate it
> to posterity; dreading to leave an illiterate ministry to the
> churches, when our present ministers shall lie in the dust.[4]

These mixed sentiments of faith and dread have always been at the heart of the college idea. They are evident at every college commencement in the eyes of parents who watch, through a screen of memories of their own receding youth, as their children advance into life. College is our American pastoral. We imagine it as a verdant world where the harshest sounds are the reciprocal thump of tennis balls or the clatter of cleats as young bodies trot up and down the fieldhouse steps. Yet bright with hope as it may be, every college is shadowed by the specter of mortality—a place where, in that uniquely American season of "fall and football

weather and the new term," the air is redolent with the "Octo-
berish smell of cured leaves."[5]

But what, exactly, is supposed to happen in this bittersweet
place—beyond sunbathing and body-toning and the competitive
exertions, athletic and otherwise, for which these are just the pre-
liminaries? First of all, it should be said that the pastoral image
of college has little to do with what most college students experience today. A few years ago, Michael S. McPherson, president
of the Spencer Foundation and former president of Macalester
College, and Morton O. Schapiro, former president of Williams
College (now of Northwestern University), pointed out that
"the nation's liberal arts college students would almost certainly
fit easily inside a Big Ten football stadium: fewer than one hundred thousand students out of more than fourteen million."[6]

Since then, the number of undergraduates has grown by
nearly a third, to around eighteen million, while the number in
liberal arts colleges—by which McPherson and Schapiro meant
a four-year residential college that is not part of a big university,
and where most students study subjects that are not narrowly
vocational such as nursing or computer programming—remains
about the same. Many college students today, of whom a growing
number are older than traditional college age, attend commuter
or online institutions focused mainly on vocational training. Often, they work and go to school at the same time, and take more
than four years to complete their degree, if they complete it at all.
Five years from now, undergraduate students in the United States
are projected to exceed twenty million, and President Obama
wants to accelerate the growth. But only a small fraction will attend college in anything like the traditional sense of the word.[7]

Whatever the context, the question remains: what's the
point? My colleague Mark Lilla put the matter well not long

ago when he spoke to the freshmen of Columbia College near the end of their first college year. He was talking, of course, to students in a college commonly described as "elite." Divided roughly equally between young men and women, these students were more racially diverse than would have been the case even a few years ago. About one in ten was born abroad or has some other claim, such as a parent with a foreign passport, to be an "international" student; and, though it's hard to tell the financial means of the students from their universal uniform of tee shirts and jeans, roughly one in seven (a somewhat higher rate than at other Ivy League colleges) is eligible for a Pell grant, a form of federal financial aid that goes to children of low-income families.

As they filed into the lecture room, they gave each other the public hugs that signify new friendships, or, in some cases, the mutually averted eyes that tell of recent breakups. They seemed simultaneously fatigued and at ease. Once they had settled into their seats, out came the iPhones and laptops, some of which stayed aglow for the whole hour, though mostly they listened, rapt. And when Lilla made the following surmise about how and why they had come to college, they reacted with the kind of quiet laughter that meant they knew he was telling the truth:

> You figured, correctly, that to be admitted you had to ex-
> ude confidence about what Americans, and only Ameri-
> cans, call their "life goals"; and you had to demonstrate
> that you have a precise plan for achieving them. It was all
> bullshit; you know that, and I know that. The real reason
> you were excited about college was because you had ques-
> tions, buckets of questions, not life plans and PowerPoint
> presentations. My students have convinced me that they

are far less interested in getting what they want than in figuring out just what it is that's worth wanting.[8]

No college teacher should presume to answer this question on behalf of the students, though, too often, he or she will try. (Requiring discipleship has always been a hazard of the teaching profession.) Instead, the job of the teacher and, collectively, of the college, is to help students in the arduous work of answering it for themselves.

To be sure, students at a college like mine have many advantages. Elite institutions confer on their students enormous benefits in the competition for positions of leadership in business, government, and higher education itself. As soon as they are admitted, even those without the prior advantage of money have already gotten a boost toward getting what they want—though not necessarily toward figuring out what's worth wanting. In fact, for some, the difficulty of that question rises in proportion to the number of choices they have. Many college students are away from their parents for the first time, although in our age of Facebook and Skype and Google Chat and the like, they are never really away. Their choices may seem limitless, but powerful forces constrain them, including what their parents want them to want. Students under financial pressure face special problems, but students from privileged families have problems too.[9]

College is supposed to be a time when such differences recede if not vanish. The notion of shared self-discovery for all students is, of course, a staple of exhortations to freshmen just coming in and valedictions to seniors about to go out—an idea invoked so often that it, too, has become a cliché. In other cultures, however, it would be an oddity. The American college has always differed fundamentally from the European university, where students are expected to know what they want (and what they are capable of) before they arrive. That is true even at the ancient English colleges of Oxford and Cambridge, to which students apply around age seventeen to "read" this or that subject, and once arrived, rarely venture outside their chosen field of formal study. By contrast, in America—in part because of our prosperity, which still exceeds that of most of the rest of the world—we try to extend the time for second chances and to defer the day when determinative choices must be made. In 1850, when Herman Melville, whose formal schooling ended at age seventeen, wrote that "a whaleship was my Yale College and my Harvard," he used the word "college" as the name of the place where (to use our modern formulation) he "found himself."

A few years ago, I came across a manuscript diary—also, as it happens, from 1850—kept by a student at a small Methodist college, Emory and Henry, in southwest Virginia. One spring evening, after attending a sermon by the college president that left him troubled and apprehensive, he made the following entry in his journal: "Oh that the Lord would show me how to think and how to choose." That sentence, poised somewhere between a wish and a plea, sounds archaic today. For many if not most students, God is no longer the object of the plea; or if he is, they probably do not attend a college where everyone worships the same god in the same way. Many American colleges began as denominational institutions; but today religion is so much a matter of private conscience, and the number of punishable infractions so small (even rules against the academic sin of plagiarism are only loosely enforced), that few college presidents would presume to intervene in the private lives of students for purposes of doctrinal or moral correction. The era of spiritual authority belonging to college is long gone. And yet I have never encountered a better formulation—"show me how to think and how to choose"—of what a college should strive to be: an aid to reflection, a place and process whereby young people take stock of their talents and passions and begin to sort out their lives in a way that is true to themselves and responsible to others.

2

Many objections can be lodged against what I have just said. For one thing, all colleges, whatever their past or present religious orientation, now exist in a context of secular pluralism that properly puts inculcation at odds with education.[10] Then there is the fact that students arrive in college already largely formed in their habits and attitudes, or, in the case of the increasing number of "nontraditional" (that is, older) students, preoccupied with the struggles of adulthood—finding or keeping a job, making or saving a marriage, doing right by one's children. Many college women, who now outnumber men, are already mothers, often single. And regardless of age or gender or social class, students experience college—in the limited sense of attending lectures, writing papers, taking exams—as a smaller part of daily life than did my generation, which came of age in the 1960s and 70s. They live now in an ocean of digital noise, logged on, online, booted up, as the phrase goes, 24/7, linked to one another through an arsenal of gadgets that are never "powered down."

Having just survived the travails of getting in, students in selective colleges find themselves under instant and constant pressure to prepare for competing with graduates of comparable colleges once they get out. Those in open-admissions colleges, many of whom must cope with deficits in their previous schooling, may not be able to compete at what we call the "same level," but they are likely to feel even more pressure to justify the cost of earning a credential in the hope that it will give them a fighting chance in postcollege life. In other words, college is less and less a respite from what my campus newspaper used to call "the real world." This is true of colleges of all types and ranks.

It may also be objected that there is nothing new about any of this—an objection with a good deal of merit. When the first administrators at Stanford (founded in 1891) wanted to know why the new freshman class had chosen to enroll, they heard mainly about the California climate, the prestige of the new university, and the (at that time) low living expenses.[11] Twenty years later, the president of Western Reserve University, a clergyman with the wonderfully donnish name Charles Thwing, found that students were less interested in "hard reading and high thinking" than in acquiring the "'touch' of college life" in order to impress prospective employers. Around the same time, at Penn State, an English professor complained of being pestered with a recurrent question about the value of what he was teaching: "Lissun, Prof, how is this dope going to help a guy get a job and pull down a good salary?"[12] And fifty years after that, the eminent critic Lionel Trilling (who taught all his life at Columbia, except for visiting stints at Harvard and Oxford) had come to feel that his students regarded college "merely as a process of accreditation, with an economic-social end in view."[13]

So it's an old and familiar story. If we look through the eyes of fiction writers who set their stories and novels on a college campus, most of what we see in the past looks a lot like the present. In Mark Twain's novel *Pudd'nhead Wilson* (1894), a young man goes up from small-town Missouri to Yale, and comes back with nothing to show except two new habits: drinking and gambling. In Edgar Allan Poe's story "William Wilson" (1839), we get a picture of the University of Virginia as a place where besotted boys indulge in round-the-clock gambling and whoring. Pretty much the same scene is described 165 years later in Tom Wolfe's novel

I Am Charlotte Simmons (2004), in which students have their mouths fastened perpetually to the spigot of a beer keg except when taking a break to have sex—though some seem capable of doing both simultaneously. And in a still more recent novel, *The Ask* (2010), by Sam Lipsyte, the narrator recalls college in the 1970s as a time when he and his housemates "drank local beer, smoked homegrown and shake":

> Senior year I moved into the House of Drinking and Smoking, took the cheap room . . . screwed a blue bulb in the ceiling and slept there, mostly alone . . . drank in the living room with . . . a crew that included . . . a guy . . . who may or may not have been a student, though by dint of his meth addiction could have counted as an apprentice chemist.[14]

Such fictions tend to be borne out by recollections of fact. In a recent oral history, the distinguished physician Spencer Foreman, who became the transformative leader of New York's Montefiore Hospital, described the small liberal arts college he attended in the 1950s as a place where "the difference between the pre-meds and the non-pre-meds" was that "the pre-meds began drinking Thursday night. Everybody else drank every night."[15] One should always be wary of accounts of college life that posit some golden age when students went to bed early and rose early, using the night to refresh themselves with sleep (solo, of course) for the lofty labors of the day to come. It has never been so.

In fact, for much of its history, college was a quasi–penal institution where boys were "sentenced" by their parents to "temporary custody."[16] Only because they could not afford to replicate the quadrangle system at Oxford and Cambridge, with its stone walls and guarded gates, did the founders of Harvard build a high fence around the yard—not so much to keep the cows and goats out as to keep the students in.[17] Today we expect the opposite: that going to college means to be released into a playground of unregulated freedom.

The most obvious instance of the expanded freedom is, of course, sex, which has come a long way from the days when it was a furtive extracurricular activity, as described in the novels of F. Scott Fitzgerald or J. P. Marquand, in which Princeton or Harvard boys, waiting to be matched with some designated debutante, find relief with prostitutes or serving-girls; or, as Philip Roth described it two generations later, when "co-eds" were "thrust up against the trunks of trees in the dark" by boys desperate in those last minutes before their dates had to return, alone, to their dorms. In most colleges, this is ancient history. A couple of years ago, the Office of Residential Life and Learning at one well-regarded northeastern college felt compelled to institute a rule banning "any sex act in a dorm room while one's roommate is present."[18] Presumably, exemption is granted to the roommate who wants to be part of the action.

Over the past half century or so, this expansion of freedom has been the most obvious change in college life—not just sexual freedom, but what might be called freedom of demeanor and deportment, freedom of choice as fields and courses have vastly multiplied, and, perhaps most important, freedom of judgment as the role of the college as arbiter of values has all but disappeared. Relatively few colleges require any particular course for graduation, and the course catalogue is likely to be somewhere between an encyclopedia and the proverbial Chinese menu— from which students choose a little of this and a little of that, unless they are majoring in one of the "hard" sciences, in which case their range of choice is much narrower.

This situation makes for certain ironies. Old institutions invoke their own antiquity in their promotional materials ("reassuring printed matter," as Thorstein Veblen described it long ago, by which "marketable illusions" are sold to the public), while within the institution, the past is denounced as a dark age of meddling trustees, autocratic presidents, and a faculty of "old boys" with benighted views of just about everything.[19] Traces of the reviled old college survived till not all that long ago. I can remember when a full-time employee of the college library patrolled the reading room tapping the shoes of students sprawled back in their chairs with their feet on the table until they sat up (or, more likely, woke up) and planted them back on the floor.

All that sort of thing has been thrown out with a hearty good riddance—and yet, as one college chaplain wrote not long ago, today's students seem to "want to retain their hard-won autonomy, while at the same time insisting that institutions assume a moral responsibility for protecting them from the consequences of that autonomy." College authorities have given up their role of acting *in loco parentis*, but when trouble breaks out over, say, some incendiary "hate speech," they still tend to get blamed for not parentally stepping in. If and when they do so, they are likely to be indulgent. Except in the "hard" sciences, academic failure, especially in elite colleges, is rare; and cheating, except in the military academies, tends to be treated as a minor lapse.

3

So college culture has undergone many deep changes—some slow to establish themselves, such as the advent of elective courses and the end of compulsory chapel in the late nineteenth century, others sudden, such as the abandonment of parietal rules in the late 1960s. There have been deep changes, too, in what some call the "learning style" of college students. The cultural critic Carlin Romano, who has taught in several colleges, reports that for many undergraduates today, being asked to read "a whole book, from A to Z, feels like a marathon unfairly imposed on a jogger"—a problem that some faculty are trying to solve by gathering students outside of class to read long works such as *Paradise Lost* or *Ulysses* aloud. The sociologist Tim Clydesdale, who teaches at the College of New Jersey, speaks of a "new epistemology," by which he means that students no longer "arrive in awe of the institution and its faculty, content to receive their education via lecture and happy to let the faculty decide what was worth knowing." Now they show up knowing "full well that authorities can be found for every position and any knowledge claim, and consequently . . . [they are] dubious (privately, that is) about anything we claim to be true or important." The Harvard English professor Louis Menand thinks that college teachers have yet to adapt the old "linear model for transmitting knowledge—the lecture monologue in which a single line of thought leads to an intellectual climax after fifty minutes—to a generation of students who are accustomed to dealing with multiple information streams in short bursts."[20] The fact is there is always a lag between what's happening in the mental world of students and that of the faculty, and by the time the latter catches up with the former, new students have arrived with new attitudes, so the cycle begins again. In the 1960s, students tended to be to the left of faculty on social and political issues. In the 2010s, it is likely to be the other way around.

Former Princeton president William Bowen keeps on his desk an alabaster calendar inscribed with a comment by the naturalist John Burroughs: "New times always! Old time we cannot keep."[21] It's good advice. And yet, in some essentials, it is also true that colleges change very little. New college presidents find out fast that they have landed in the slowest-changing institutions in American life—slower, even, than the post office. The Ohio University economist Richard Vedder gets reliable laughs when he tells corporate audiences that "with the possible exception of prostitution, teaching is the only profession that has had absolutely no productivity advance in the 2400 years since Socrates." Shortly before the economic debacle of 2008, former president of Johns Hopkins William Brody remarked that "if you went to a [college] class circa 1900, and you went today, it would look exactly the same, while if you went to an automobile plant in 1900 and today, you wouldn't recognize the place."[22]

It may well be true that the strongest force in academia is inertia. But, contrary to his intention, Vedder's joke could be construed to mean that neither prostitution nor teaching can be improved through economies of scale; and Brody's invidious comparison was badly timed, since a few months later the auto companies (except for Ford) came within a whisker of going belly up, while our colleges more or less weathered the storm. His comment also wasn't exactly accurate, since in the college classroom of 1900 you would probably have seen no women unless you were visiting one of the new women's colleges; nor would you have seen any persons of color, unless you were visiting, say, Tuskegee or Howard or Morehouse. What is true is that the method of teaching in 1900 was pretty much the same as it is now: no PowerPoint, different dress code—but otherwise recognizable.

And so, I think, are the students. They have always been searching for purpose. They have always been unsure of their gifts and goals, and susceptible to the demands—overt and covert—of their parents and of the abstraction we call "the market." There is much talk today, as well there should be, about students resorting to cheating or binge drinking in response to these pressures, while others fall into chronic anxiety and depression. It is probably true that these problems have grown in recent years, along with our awareness of them.[23] But lest we think that something altogether new is happening, consider this passage from an 1871 novel by Harriet Beecher Stowe, written in the voice of a man thinking back to his senior year:

> During my last year, the question, "What are you good for?" had often borne down like a nightmare upon me. When I entered college all was distant, golden, indefinite, and I was sure that I was good for almost anything that could be named. Nothing that had ever been attained by man looked to me impossible. Riches, honor, fame, anything that any other man unassisted had wrought out for himself with his own right arm, I could work out also.
>
> But as I measured myself with real tasks, and as I rubbed and grated against other minds and whirled round and round in the various experiences of college life, I grew smaller and smaller in my own esteem, and oftener and oftener in my lonely hours it seemed as if some evil genius delighted to lord it over me and sitting at my bed-side or fire-side to say "What are you good for, to what purpose all the pains and money that have been thrown away on you? You'll never be anything; you'll only mortify your poor mother that has set her heart on you, and make your Uncle Job ashamed of you." Can any anguish equal the depths of those blues in which a man's whole self hangs in suspense before his own eyes, and he doubts whether he himself, with his entire outfit and apparatus, body, soul, and spirit, isn't to be, after all,

a complete failure? Better, he thinks never to have been born, than to be born to no purpose. . . .[24]

With a few small changes in diction, these sentences could have been written today. Now, as then, most students have no clear conception of why or to what end they are in college. Some students have always been aimless, bored, or confused; others self-possessed, with their eyes on the prize. Most are somewhere in between, looking for something to care about.

What does all this mean for those (students, faculty, administrators, alumni, donors, legislators, trustees) who have something to say about what happens in America's colleges? Surely it means that every college has an obligation to make itself a place not just for networking and credentialing but for learning in the broad and deep meaning of that word. It means that all students deserve something more from college than semi-supervised fun or the services of an employment agency. Good colleges can still be transformative in the sense of the title of a best-selling book, *Colleges that Change Lives*, which has become a welcome alternative to the usual guides (*Barron's, Princeton Review, U.S. News & World Report*), which simply list colleges in a hierarchy of prestige that conforms almost exactly to the relative size of their endowments.

For all these reasons, it is particularly painful when those colleges at the top of the usual lists, the ones with the most resources and (as they like to claim) the most talent, fail to confront their obligations—when, as the former dean of Harvard College, Harry Lewis, puts it, they "affect horror" that "students attend college in the hope of becoming financially successful, but . . . offer students neither a coherent view of the point of a college education nor any guidance on how they might discover for themselves some larger purpose in life." Lewis's critique of "the service-station conception" of college is more than a gripe at his home institution.[25] It is a call for every college to do what every true teacher, at least since Socrates, has asked every student to do: engage in some serious self-examination.

4

What, then, are today's prevailing answers to the question, what is college for? There are basically three. The most common answer is an economic one, though it is really two linked answers: first, that providing more people with a college education is good for the economic health of the nation; and, second, that going to college is good for the economic competitiveness of the individuals who constitute the nation.

Politicians tend to emphasize the first point, as when Richard Riley, secretary of education under President Clinton, said in a much-quoted comment that we must educate our workers for an increasingly unpredictable future: "We are currently preparing students for jobs that don't yet exist using technologies that haven't been invented in order to solve problems that we don't even know are problems yet." President Obama makes the same point more briefly: "countries that out-teach us today will out-compete us tomorrow."[26]

As for the second economic rationale—the competitiveness of individuals—it's clear that a college degree long ago supplanted the high school diploma as the minimum qualification for entry into the skilled labor market, and there is abundant evidence that people with a college degree earn more money over the course of their lives than people without one. One authority claims that those who hold a BA degree earn roughly 60 percent more, on average, over their lifetime than those who do not. Some estimates put the worth of a BA degree at about a million dollars in incremental lifetime earnings. More conservative analysts, taking account of the cost of obtaining the degree, arrive at a more modest number, but there is little dispute that one reason to go to college is to increase one's earning power.[27]

For such economic reasons alone, it is alarming that the United States has been slipping relative to other developed nations as measured by the percentage of its younger population with at least some postsecondary education. There are differences of opinion about how much we have slipped, but there is general agreement that American leadership in higher education is in jeopardy and can no longer be taken for granted. For the first time in our history, we face the prospect that the coming generation of adult Americans will be less educated than their elders.[28]

Within this gloomy general picture are some especially disturbing particulars. For one thing, flat or declining college attainment rates (relative to other nations) apply disproportionately to minorities, who are a growing portion of the American population. And financial means has a shockingly large bearing on educational opportunity, which, according to one authority, looks like this in today's America: if you are the child of a family making more than $90,000 per year, your odds of getting a BA by age twenty-four are roughly one in two; if your family's income is between $60,000 and $90,000, your odds are roughly one in four; if your parents make less than $35,000, your odds are one in seventeen.[29]

Moreover, among those who do get to college, high-achieving students from affluent families are four times more likely to attend a selective college than students from poor families with comparable grades and test scores.[30] And since prestigious colleges (prestige correlates almost exactly with selectivity) serve as funnels into leadership positions in business, law, and government, this means that our "best" colleges are doing more to sustain than to retard the growth of inequality in our society. Yet colleges are still looked to as engines of social mobility in American life, and it would be shameful if they became, even more than they already are, a system for replicating inherited wealth.

Not surprisingly, as in any discussion of economic matters, one finds dissenters from the predominant view. Some on the right say that pouring more public investment into higher education, in the form of enhanced subsidies for individuals or institutions, is a bad idea. They say that the easy availability of government funds is one reason for inflation in the price of tuition. They argue against the goal of universal college education as a fond fantasy and, instead, for a sorting system such as one finds in European countries, where children are directed according to test results early in life toward the kind of schooling deemed suitable for them: vocational training for the low-scorers, who will be the semiskilled laborers and functionaries; advanced education for the high-scorers, who will be the diplomats and doctors, and so on.[31]

Others, on the left, question whether the aspiration to go to college really makes sense for "low-income students who can least afford to spend money and years" on such a risky venture, given their low graduation rates and high debt. Such skeptics point out, too, that most new jobs likely to be created over the next decade will probably not require a college degree. From this point of view, the "education gospel" seems a cruel distraction from "what really provides security to families and children: good jobs at fair wages, robust unions, affordable access to health care and transportation."[32]

One can be on either side of these questions, or somewhere in the middle, and still believe in the goal of achieving universal college education. Consider an analogy from another sphere of public debate: health care. One sometimes hears that eliminating smoking would save untold billions because of the immense cost of caring for patients who develop lung cancer, emphysema, heart disease, or diabetes—among the many diseases caused or exacerbated by smoking. It turns out, however, that reducing the incidence of disease by curtailing smoking (one of the major public-health successes of recent decades) may actually end up costing us more, since people who don't smoke live longer, and eventually require expensive therapies for chronic diseases and the inevitable infirmities of old age. Yet who does not think it a good thing when a person stops smoking and thereby improves his or her chances of living a longer and healthier life? In other words, measuring the benefit as a social cost or social gain does not quite get the point—or at least not the whole point. The best reason to end smoking is that people who don't smoke have a better chance to lead better lives.[33] The best reason to care about college—who goes, and what happens to them when they get there—is not what it does for society in economic terms but what it can do for individuals, in both calculable and incalculable ways.

5

The second argument for the importance of college is a political one, though one rarely hears it from politicians. This is the argument on behalf of democracy. "The basis of our government," as Thomas Jefferson put the matter near the end of the eighteenth century, is "the opinion of the people." And so if the new republic was to flourish and endure, it required, above all, an educated citizenry—a conviction in which Jefferson was joined by John Adams, who disagreed with him on just about everything else, but who concurred that "the whole people must take upon themselves the education of the whole people, and must be willing to bear the expense of it."[34]

This is more true than ever. All of us are bombarded every day with pleadings and persuasions, of which many are distortions and deceptions—advertisements, political appeals, punditry of all sorts—designed to capture our loyalty, money, or, more narrowly, our vote. Some say health-care reform will bankrupt the country, others that it is an overdue act of justice; some believe that abortion is the work of Satan, others think that to deny a woman the right to terminate an unwanted pregnancy is a form of abuse; some assure us that charter schools are the salvation of a broken school system, others are equally sure that they violate the public trust; some regard nuclear energy as our best chance to break free from fossil fuels, others describe it, especially in the wake of the tsunami in Japan, as Armageddon waiting to happen. Any such list could be extended indefinitely with conflicting claims between which citizens must choose or somehow mediate, so it should be obvious that the best chance we have to maintain a functioning democracy is a citizenry that can tell the difference between demagoguery and responsible arguments.

About a hundred years ago, a professor of moral philosophy at Oxford, John Alexander Smith, got to the nub of the matter. "Gentleman," he said to the incoming class (the students were all men in those days), "Nothing that you will learn in the course of your studies will be of the slightest possible use to you in after life—save only this—that if you work hard and intelligently you should be able to detect when a man is talking rot, and that, in my view, is the main, if not the sole, purpose of education."[35] Americans tend to prefer a two-syllable synonym, bullshit, for the one-syllable Anglicism, rot—and so we might say that the most important thing one can acquire in college is a well-functioning bullshit meter.[36] It's a technology that will never become obsolete.

Putting it this way may sound flippant, but a serious point is at stake: education for democracy not only requires extending educational opportunity but also implies something about what kind of education democratic citizens need. A very good case for college in this sense has been made recently by former Yale Law School dean Anthony Kronman, who now teaches in a Great Books program for Yale undergraduates. In a book with the double-entendre title, *Education's End: Why Our Colleges and Universities Have Given Up on the Meaning of Life*, Kronman argues for a course of study (at Yale it is voluntary; at my college, Columbia, it is compulsory) that introduces students to the constitutive ideas of Western culture. At Yale, relatively few students, about 10 percent of the entering class, are admitted to this program, which is called "Directed Studies." At Columbia, the "Core Curriculum" is required of all students, which has the advantage, since they are randomly assigned to sections (currently capped at twenty-two), of countering their tendency to associate mainly with classmates from the same socioeconomic or ethnic background, or in their own major or club or fraternity house. The Core also counters the provincialism of the faculty. Senior and junior professors, along with graduate student instructors, gather weekly to discuss the assigned texts—a rare opportunity for faculty from different fields, and at different stages of their careers, to consider substantive questions. And, not least among its benefits, it links all students in the college to one another through a body of common knowledge: once they have gone through the Core, no student is a complete stranger to any other.

Whether such a curriculum is an option or an obligation, its value is vividly evident in Kronman's enumeration of the ideas it raises for discussion and debate:

The ideals of individual freedom and toleration; of democratic government; of respect for the rights of minorities and for human rights generally; a reliance on markets as a mechanism for the organization of economic life and a recognition of the need for markets to be regulated by a supervenient political authority; a reliance, in the political realm, on the methods of bureaucratic administration, with its formal division of functions and legal separation of office from officeholder; an acceptance of the truths of modern science and the ubiquitous employment of its technological products: all these provide, in many parts of the world, the existing foundations of political, social, and economic life, and where they do not, they are viewed as aspirational goals toward which everyone has the strongest moral and material reasons to strive.[37]

Anyone who earns a BA from a reputable college ought to understand something about the genealogy of these ideas and practices, about the historical processes from which they have emerged, the tragic cost when societies fail to defend them, and about alternative ideas both within the Western tradition and outside it. That's a tall order for anyone to satisfy on his or her own—and one of the marks of an educated person is the recognition that it can never be adequately done and is therefore all the more worth doing.

6

Both of these cases for college—the argument for national and individual competitiveness, and the argument for inclusive democratic citizenship—are serious and compelling. But there is a third case, more rarely heard, perhaps because it is harder to articulate without sounding platitudinous and vague. I first heard

it stated in a plain and passionate way after I had spoken to an
alumni group from the college in which I teach. I had been com-
mending Columbia's core curriculum—which, in addition to
two yearlong courses in literary and philosophical classics, also
requires the study of art and music for one semester each. Recently, a new course called "Frontiers of Science," designed to ensure that students leave college with some basic understanding of
contemporary scientific developments, has been added. The emphasis in my talk was on the Jeffersonian argument—education
for citizenship. When I had finished, an elderly alumnus stood
up and said more or less the following: "That's all very nice, professor, but you've missed the main point." With some trepida-
tion, I asked him what that point might be. "Columbia," he said,
"taught me how to enjoy life."

What he meant was that college had opened his senses as well
as his mind to experiences that would otherwise be foreclosed for
him. Not only his capacity to read demanding works of literature
and to grasp fundamental political ideas, but also his alertness to
color and form, melody and harmony, had been heightened and
deepened—and now, in the late years of his life, he was grateful.
Such an education is a hedge against utilitarian values. It has no
room for dogma—only for debate about the meaning, or meanings, of truth. It slakes the human craving for contact with works
of art that somehow register one's own longings and yet exceed
what one has been able to articulate by and for oneself. As the
gentleman reminded me, it is among the invaluable experiences
of the fulfilled life, and surely our colleges have an obligation to
coax and prod students toward it.

If all that seems too pious or earnest, I think of a comparably
personal comment I once heard my colleague Judith Shapiro, former provost of Bryn Mawr and then president of Barnard, make

to a group of young people about what they should expect from college: "You want the inside of your head to be an interesting place to spend the rest of your life." What both Judith and the Columbia alum were talking about is sometimes called "liberal education"—a hazardous term today since it has nothing necessarily to do with liberal politics in the modern sense of the word. (Former Beloit College president Victor Ferrall suggests scrapping that troublesome adjective and replacing it with something bland like "broad, open, inclusive," or simply "general.")[38] The phrase *liberal education* derives from the classical tradition of *artes liberales*, which was reserved in Greece and Rome—where women were considered inferior and slavery was an accepted feature of civilized society—for "those free men or gentlemen possessed of the requisite leisure for study."[39] Conserved by medieval scholastics, renewed in the scholarly resurgence we call the Renaissance, and again in the Enlightenment, the tradition of liberal learning survived and thrived in Europe, but remained largely the possession of ruling elites.

Seen in this long view, the distinctive American contribution has been the attempt to democratize it, to deploy it on behalf of the cardinal American principle that all persons, regardless of origin, have the right to pursue happiness—and that "getting to know," in Matthew Arnold's much-quoted phrase, "the best which has been thought and said in the world" is helpful to that pursuit. This view of what it means to be educated is often caricatured as snobbish and narrow, beholden to the old and wary of the new; but in fact it is neither, as Arnold makes clear by the (seldom quoted) phrase with which he completes his point: "and through this knowledge, turning a stream of fresh and free thought upon our stock notions and habits."[40] In other words, knowledge of the past helps us to think critically about the present.

Arguably the most eloquent defense of liberal education remains that of Arnold's contemporary John Henry Newman in *The Idea of a University* (1852), where, in a definition that encompasses science as well as what is customarily called the "humanities," he describes liberal knowledge as "knowledge which stands on its own pretensions, which is independent of sequel, expects no complement, refuses to be *informed* (as it is called) by any end, or absorbed into any art, in order duly to present itself to our contemplation."[41] In today's America, at every kind of institution—from underfunded community colleges to the wealthiest Ivies—this kind of education is at risk. Students are pressured and programmed, trained to live from task to task, relentlessly rehearsed and tested until winners are culled from the rest. They scarcely have time for what Newman calls contemplation, and too many colleges do too little to save them from the debilitating frenzy that makes liberal education marginal or merely ornamental—if it is offered at all.[42]

In this respect, notwithstanding the bigotries and prejudices of earlier generations, we might not be so quick to say that today's colleges mark an advance over those of the past. Consider a once-popular college novel written a hundred years ago, *Stover at Yale* (1912), in which the young Yalie declares, "I'm going to do the best thing a fellow can do at our age, I'm going to loaf."[43] Stover speaks from the immemorial past, and what he says is likely to sound to us today like a sneering boast from the idle rich. But there is a more dignified sense in which "loaf" is the colloquial equivalent of what Newman meant by contemplation, and has always been part of the promise of American life. "I loaf and invite my soul," says Walt Whitman in that great democratic poem *Song of Myself*, "I lean and loaf at my ease observing a spear of summer grass."

Surely, every American college ought to defend this waning possibility, whatever we call it. And an American college is only true to itself when it opens its doors to all—rich, middling, and poor—who have the capacity to embrace the precious chance to think and reflect before life engulfs them. If we are serious about democracy, that means everyone.

TWO
ORIGINS

The assumption that young adults should pass through a period of higher education before entering a life of commerce or service is, of course, much older than the United States and older, too, than the English colonies that became the United States. Aristotle identified the years between puberty and age twenty-one as the formative time for mind and character, and it was customary for young Greek men to attend a series of lectures that resembled our notion of a college "course." In Augustan Rome, gatherings of students under instruction by settled teachers took on some of the attributes we associate with modern colleges (libraries, fraternities, organized sports), and, by the Middle Ages, efforts to regulate the right to teach by issuing licenses were under way in such nascent educational centers as Paris and Padua—presaging the modern idea of a faculty with exclusive authority to grant degrees.[1] In short, college in the broad sense of the term has a history that exceeds two millennia.

But college as we know it is fundamentally an English idea. It was brought to New England early in the seventeenth century by English Protestants who left home in dissent from the established church. To these "Puritans" (as their enemies called them, on account of their putative severity of mind and spirit), education was vitally important, and while they drew upon ancient and medieval precedents, they had particularly in mind their own experience in the colleges of Cambridge and Oxford.

Founded in the thirteenth century, the earliest English colleges were essentially retreats for scholars of divinity whose duties included celebrating mass for the soul of the benefactor who had endowed the college and thereby spared them from menial work. In today's terms, we might say that the first colleges were groups of graduate students on fellowship.[2] But by the fifteenth century, it had become common for the resident scholars to supply or supplement their living by giving instruction and accommodation to younger students whom we would call undergraduates. These boarders (or, as they were known at Cambridge, pensioners) were sometimes kinsmen of the college benefactor, or candidates admitted on the recommendation of some trusted schoolmaster who spoke for their character and competence in Latin. There were no entrance examinations.

Vouched for or not, undergraduates were guarded and watched since students then, no less than now, were not reliably compliant with the wishes of parents or patrons. One visitor to seventeenth-century Cambridge was shocked to witness "swearing, drinking, rioting, and hatred of all piety and virtue" among the students, who could not be trusted to obey the college rules, including the prohibition against "fierce birds" in their rooms. A few years earlier, a student mob jammed the Great Hall of Trinity

College, smoking, hissing, and throwing pellets at the actors who displeased them in a play written by one of the Trinity fellows.[3]

By the later fifteenth century, the cloistered structure of the Oxbridge college had emerged in its modern form: rooms accessible from an inner courtyard connected by walkways to chapel, library, and hall. The hall—a great room with rushes strewn on the floor to be gathered up and burned from time to time as a means of controlling dirt—was the center of college life. It was in hall that dining, lectures, and sometimes musical and theatrical performances took place; at one end stood the "high table," where tutors dined in the company of the Master, who, as the only college official permitted to marry, lived with his family in an attached house.[4] Part of the point—an important part—was for undergraduates to witness social and intellectual exchange among their superiors, in the hope that they would aspire someday to be worthy of sitting among them.

To this end, the initiates, or, to use the penal metaphor, the inmates, were kept in, and the public kept out. Traffic flowed through a single point of entrance and exit, the porter's gate.[5] The student's day began with predawn worship, followed by lectures, study, and meditation in what was in some respects a monastic regime of discipline and deprivation. This was the stringent world that produced John Milton and Oliver Cromwell (who toughened himself at football in the courtyard of Sidney Sussex College, Cambridge) and, a little later, Isaac Newton.

But if it was a strict and confined world, it was also coddled and collegial—the latter adjective, like the noun "college," derives from the Latin *collegium*, meaning society or community—in which young men, denied the pleasures of tavern and town, were offered recreation in the college gardens, bowling green, tennis court, bathing pool, or archery range.[6] Among the roughly 20,000 persons who emigrated to New England in the 1630s, nearly 150 were graduates of one of these institutions—better than 1 in every 75 men, a ratio comparable to the college-educated percentage of Americans up until the twentieth century. The college with by far the highest representation (35 graduates or affiliates) was Emmanuel College, founded at Cambridge in the late sixteenth century on what Queen Elizabeth presciently called "a Puritan foundation." Emmanuel turned out to be the Old English "oak" to the New England sapling planted by Puritan emigrants in 1636 at Newtowne, soon renamed Cambridge in honor of the English university town. To this fledgling New England college a Puritan merchant and Emmanuel graduate named John Harvard bequeathed half his estate and all his library.[7]

In the fund-raising request they sent to prospective donors back in England, the founders of the new college thanked God for seeing fit "to stir up the heart of Mr. Harvard," and by way of asking others to follow his example, explained the purpose for which they intended to use his books and funds: to "advance learning and perpetuate it to posterity." The kind of learning they had in mind was, among others, theological learning. In what they would have called a providential mercy, the only book from John Harvard's library to survive an eighteenth-century fire was a tract entitled *Christian Warfare.*[8]

But it is a mistake to imagine the first American colleges as seminaries devoted solely to doctrine and dogma. Fewer than half of Harvard's seventeenth-century graduates ultimately entered the ministry, and the study of logic and ethics—classical as well as Christian—took up a considerable part of the students' attention, as did arithmetic and geometry.[9] Another early appeal for funds, this one specifically for the Harvard library, enumerated the need for volumes on "law, phisicke, Philosophy, and Mathematics," and along with Augustine's *City of God* and Calvin's *Institutes*, library holdings included Erasmus's *Colloquies* and even the bawdy comedies of the Roman playwright Plautus.[10] In short, the American college was conceived from the start as more than narrowly ecclesiastical, with the larger aim, as the historian Samuel Eliot Morison put it, to "develop the whole man—his body and soul as well as his intellect" toward the formation of a person inclined to "unity, gentility, and public service."

Religion, to be sure, came first. To study the Bible was to learn to parse God's word—no small task, since, in what Christians called the Old Testament, God spoke through shadows ("types" or "*umbra*") of truths as yet unrevealed, and, in the New Testament, through parables and prophecies requiring informed interpretation. Yet the Bible did not contain all God's truth. God also expressed his punitive or protective will through historical events (pilgrimages, holy wars) and judgments of nature (flood, earthquake, drought). And he conferred on all human beings the capacity for responsive pleasure at natural intimations of his supernatural excellence such as the celestial dance of sun, moon, and stars, the symmetrical beauty of plants and trees, or the ripples that flow outward in perfect circles when a stone is thrown into tranquil water. God furnished the natural world with what Jonathan Edwards (Yale, class of 1720; appointed president of Princeton in 1758) called "beauties that delight us and we can't tell why"—as when "we find ourselves pleased in beholding the color of the violets, but we know not what secret regularity or harmony it is that creates that pleasure in our minds."[11]

The early American college required its students to study not only scriptural texts and commentaries, but also history and natural philosophy—a tripartite division of knowledge corresponding roughly to today's triumvirate of humanities, social sciences, and natural sciences. A college aspired to be a place (in Newman's later formulation) where "all branches of knowledge" are "connected together, because the subject-matter of knowledge is intimately united in itself, as being the acts and the work of the Creator." Its subject was nothing less, in Edwards's words, than "the university of things," a phrase that preserves the root meaning of the word "university": the gathering of all knowledge into a unified whole. Until the last third of the nineteenth century, this effort to grasp what Frederick Barnard (the man for whom the women's college at my university was named) called "the beautiful truths which are to be read in the works of God" remained the official purpose of America's colleges.[12]

Today, the word "interdisciplinary" is bandied about at every academic conference and praised in every dean's report, but in fact most of our academic institutions are much less interdisciplinary than were their counterparts in the past. In the early American college, since all studies were unified as one integrated study of the divine mind, boundaries between "fields" or "disciplines" did not exist. "There is not one truth in religion, another in mathematics, and a third in physics and in art," as one Harvard graduate (class of 1825) put the matter. "There is one truth, even as one God."[13]

2

Yet this dream of what some today would call "consilience" did not exhaust the meaning of the college idea. For the Puritans, according to Morison,

> university learning apart from college life was not worth
> having; and the humblest resident tutor was accounted a
> more suitable teacher than the most eminent community

lecturer. Book learning alone might be got by lectures and reading; but it was only by studying and disputing, eating and drinking, playing and praying as members of the same collegiate community, in close and constant association with each other and with their tutors, that the priceless gift of character could be imparted to young men.

Already in his own day (Morison was writing nearly seventy-five years ago), the man who wrote these words was deliberately anachronistic. Even after motorcars had become commonplace, he liked to travel on horseback from his home on Beacon Hill to Harvard Yard, where he tethered his mount to a hitching post before lecturing in riding boots. And even when the "old-time college," as historians sometimes call it, gave way to the modern university, the appeal to character persisted in official pronouncements of what the university was all about. Writing in 1886, the founding president of Johns Hopkins, an institution mainly devoted to advanced research where undergraduates were initially absent, insisted that a university must never be "merely a place for the advancement of knowledge or for the acquisition of learning; it will always be a place for the development of character."[14]

Today, this assertion that a college should concern itself with something called character will strike us as a throwback to another time and world. Character, moreover, is a word with a confusing history. It has been used as a synonym for probity, but also for sheer stamina—as when Nobel laureate Arthur Lewis spoke, at his installation as chancellor of the University of Guyana, of character as the determination "to practice the same thing over and over again, while others are enjoying themselves; to push oneself from the easy part to the hard part; to listen to criticism and use it; to reject one's own work and try again."[15]

Sometimes the word has been put to unsavory uses. By the early twentieth century, it had become a thinly disguised term of discrimination between the model Protestant gentleman and the putatively grasping parvenu—in particular, the importunate Jew—knocking on the college door. During Morison's undergraduate years, Harvard's president, Abbott Lawrence Lowell, proposed "a personal estimate of character on the part of the Admission authorities" in order to control the "dangerous increase in the proportion of Jews" (the top floor of one dormitory had become unaffectionately known as "Kike's Peak").[16] And even in the absence of overt bigotry, judgments of "character" tend to boil down to how comfortable the judge feels in the presence of the judged. In a letter to Lowell, Harvard alumnus Judge Learned Hand demurred from the president's plan for screening out undesirables: "If anyone could devise an honest test for character," Hand wrote, "perhaps it would serve well. I doubt its feasibility except to detect formal and obvious delinquencies. Short of it, it seems to me that students can only be chosen by tests of scholarship, unsatisfactory as those no doubt are. . . ."[17] If the "newer races," as they were sometimes referred to, were outperforming the old boys in grades and scores, then so be it: let them in.

Yet despite its history of misuse and abuse, there is something worth conserving in the claim, as Newman put it, that education "implies an action upon our mental nature, and the formation of a character."[18] College, more than brain-training for this or that functional task, *should* be concerned with character—the attenuated modern word for what the founders of our first colleges would have called soul or heart. Although we may no longer agree on the attributes of virtue as codified in biblical commandments or, for that matter, in Enlightenment precepts (Jefferson thought the aim of education was to produce citizens capable of "temperate liberty"), students still come to college not yet fully formed as social beings, and may still be deterred from sheer self-interest toward a life of enlarged sympathy and civic responsibility.

This idea that the aim of education includes fostering ethical as well as analytical intelligence long predates the churches from which the early American colleges arose, and is, of course, much older than Christianity itself. In the *Beit Midrash* of ancient Judaism, typically located physically as well as spiritually near the synagogue, students prayed for insight and clarity of mind before embarking on the day's Torah study. To join Plato's academy in Athens of the fourth-century BCE was to acknowledge "a change of heart and the adoption of a new way of life via a process akin to our own understanding of religious conversion."[19] In first-century Rome, in Seneca's famous letter on the purpose of learning, we find a measured yet passionate account of the power of liberal education to clear the mind of cant by inviting it to rise above the palaver of everyday life as well as above pedantry:

> We have no leisure to hear lectures on the question
> whether [Ulysses] was sea-tost between Italy and Sicily,
> or outside our known world. . . . We ourselves encounter
> storms of the spirit, which toss us daily, and our deprav-
> ity drives us into all the ills which troubled Ulysses. . . .
> Show me rather, by the example of Ulysses, how I am
> to love my country, my wife, my father, and how, even
> after suffering shipwreck, I am to sail toward these ends,
> honourable as they are. Why try to discover whether
> Penelope was a pattern of purity, or whether she had the
> laugh on her contemporaries? Or whether she suspected
> that the man in her presence was Ulysses, before she
> knew it was he? Teach me rather what purity is, and how

great a good we have in it, and whether it is situated in the body or in the soul.[20]

Whether expressed in Hebrew, Greek, Roman, Christian, or the secular terms of modernity, none of these educational aspirations gainsays the obvious fact that all lives are shaped by a mysterious confluence of innate disposition and external influence, over which no institution can possibly exert complete control. Yet the fact that students can be touched and inspired as well as trained and informed has always been the true teacher's aim and joy. In America, where this view of education has been held by traditionalists and progressives alike, Emerson gave it memorable expression when he wrote in his journal that "the whole secret of the teacher's force lies in the conviction that men are convertible. And they are. They want awakening." Teachers have always been—and, let us hope, always will be—in the business of trying to "get the soul out of bed, out of her deep habitual sleep."[21]

3

When we turn from teachers to students, another striking continuity over the long history of college comes into view: their age has stayed relatively constant. More than four hundred years ago, the English scholastic Roger Ascham proposed that the ideal time to begin college is at seventeen. Some two and half centuries later, the average age of Harvard freshmen was sixteen and a half. Fifty years after that, at Yale, the average had crept up to eighteen, widely considered to be "the normal age, under reasonably favorable conditions" for college matriculation.[22]

There has been continuity, too, in the way educators describe the stages that young people pass through en route to intellectual and ethical maturity. In this respect, Puritans made little distinction between college and church. Both institutions existed to serve human beings at war with themselves, tainted by original sin yet harboring the seed of grace—divided, that is, between the will to pride and self-love and the impulse to humility and selfless-ness. Puritans spoke longingly of the change that can save these creatures from themselves by opening their minds and hearts to hitherto incomprehensible contradictions such as "God's justice mixed with his mercy" as well as their own powerlessness and perseverance—in short, to the paradoxical nature of existence in all its boundedness and boundlessness. To be educated in this sense—in the root sense, that is, of the Latin *ex ducere*, to lead forth, or, according to an alternative Latin source, *educare*, to rear or bring up children—is to be enlarged by "new affections, and new language," freed from the limits of jealous self-regard in which one has hitherto been confined. "Education," as Emerson summed up the matter, amounts to "drawing out the soul."[23]

Almost a century and a half later, the educational psychologist William Perry, in describing the ideal trajectory from freshman to senior year, offered what was essentially a translation of these first principles. A true education, he believed (as paraphrased by another distinguished educational psychologist, L. Lee Knefel-kamp), is one whereby the college student learns to "accommo-date uncertainty, paradox, and the demands of greater complex-ity." The process, Perry wrote, "begins with simplistic forms in which a person construes his world in unqualified polar terms of absolute right-wrong, good-bad; it ends with those complex forms through which he undertakes to affirm his own commit-ments in a world of contingent knowledge and relative values."[24] The terms of description may have changed, but even as it allows for the relativism of modern life, this account of the psychological and ethical growth of college students is remarkably congruent with much earlier views of what college is for. More than achieving the competence to solve problems and perform complex tasks, education means attaining and sustaining curiosity and humility. It means growing out of an embattled sense of self into a more generous view of life as continuous self-reflection in light of new experience, including the witnessed experience of others.

With these ends in view, Puritans spoke almost indistinguishably about teaching and preaching. Consider John Cotton, arguably the leading minister of New England's first generation. In his history of early New England, the *Magnalia Christi Americana* (1702), Cotton Mather (Cotton's grandson), portrays him as a man whose religious faith and scholarly attainment are essentially one and the same. A "*universal scholar*, and a *living system* of the liberal arts, and a *walking library*," he was the very ideal to which every studious young person should aspire. His reputation as a preacher was that of a man not merely erudite and eloquent but also able to inspire young people so they might "be fitted for public service."[25] By his voice and arguments, but most of all by his manifest commitment to the impossible yet imperative task of aligning his own life with models of virtue that he found (mainly) in scripture, he was mentor to his students in the same way that he was pastor to his flock. In his theological writings, which were largely concerned with what we would call moral psychology, he explored the mystery and contingency of learning, which, he believed, sometimes proceeds in steps, sometimes by leaps, sometimes by sheer surprise in the absence of exertion, sometimes by slow and arduous accretion through diligent work.

Such a teacher is convinced that everyone has the capacity to learn and grow, but that the moment of electric connection between teacher and student cannot be predicted or planned. For some students it may never come ("some go all the way through college," as Perry put it, "and somehow manage to remain school-boys to the end"); for others it may come when least expected.[26] In order to create the best conditions for it to take hold, such a teacher avoids exhibitionistic erudition, speaks in plain rather than florid language, and, humble before the subject, under-stands himself as merely the human instrument by which God *may* choose to convey to the student the "spirit of discernment." Such a teacher also knows there is no telling when, or whether, the transmission will take place.

In our mostly post-theistic academic world, these assumptions may seem remote and possibly bizarre—but perhaps they are less so than they appear. Every true teacher, after all, understands that, along with teacher and students, a mysterious third force is present in every classroom. Sometimes this force works in favor of learning; sometimes it works against it. This is because ideas must cross an invisible interval between the mind of the teacher and that of the student, and there is no telling when a provoking thought will succeed in crossing that space, or what exactly will happen to it during its transit from speaker to hearer. One never knows how the teacher's voice will be received by the student, in whose mind it mixes with already-resident ideas that have accu-mulated from prior experience and, perhaps, from other teachers. Sometimes the spoken word is nothing but noise that evaporates into air or has no effect in the mind of the student beyond annoy-ance or confusion. Sometimes it can have surprising and powerful effects—yet it is impossible to say why or when this will happen for some students and not for others.

The Puritan word for this invisible and inaudible force was grace. One does not need to share their belief—or to be a be-liever in any conventional sense—to understand what they meant. To explain their concept of grace to my own students (the rare student at my college who comes from an evangelical background needs no explanation), I sometimes draw an analogy from outside the classroom. Imagine that two college roommates go out together to see a production of Shakespeare's great play, *King Lear*, about an old man cruelly duped by his own children, who is losing his grip on power and dignity and even his own senses, and ends up wandering alone under the open sky without shelter or mercy or hope. The roommates go to see a local production of the play, and when it is done, one of them comes out of the theater saying, "You know, I've seen it done better; let's get a beer," or, "I don't know what all the fuss is about; this guy had it coming, he's a real whiner."

Meanwhile, the other young man has had a devastating experience. He doesn't know why or how, but he finds himself thinking about his own father—about the obligations of children to parents and, for that matter, parents to children; about the savage sadness that comes upon many people in their broken old age; in fact, he finds himself thinking about every aspect of his life in a new way. Does he want to have children of his own? If so, how will he bring them up? Maybe he thinks about becoming a physician; or maybe he's decided to call home to see how his father is doing, with whom he's had a difficult relationship; or, more likely, he doesn't know what to do but feels a sudden conviction that his plans and priorities need to be revisited and revised. One thing he knows for sure is that he doesn't want to end up like Lear wandering alone on the heath. In short, the world has been transformed for him while it remains utterly unchanged for his friend. And yet they have heard the same voices and words, seen the same bodies and props moving about on the same stage, or, to put it in mechanistic terms, experienced the same aural and visual stimuli.

It is impossible to say why something so important has happened to one of these young men and not to the other. Their SAT scores may be identical. In fact, the one whom the play leaves unmoved may have higher scores and better grades and better prospects to make the dean's list. The difference between them is immeasurable by any testing instrument, and has nothing to do with which one has studied harder for tomorrow's exam on Elizabethan drama. While most of us who work in education today have no language to account for this mystery, that does not mean the mystery does not exist.

Such inexplicable human differences were of intense interest to the founders of America's first colleges, and sometimes their efforts to elucidate the differences run closer than we might expect to what we are likely to think today. They believed, for instance, that learning can be blocked by pride (in either teacher or student), and that it can also be blocked by shame. Today, social psychologists speak of "stereotype threat" to explain low academic achievement by minority students who may have been distrusted or demeaned by adults as well as peers ever since they can remember. Some such students, knowing they are expected to do poorly or to fail, find themselves fulfilling that expectation in spite of talent and effort. It's a phenomenon that researchers have shown to be widespread, and is closely akin to what one seventeenth-century minister had in mind when he told his congregation that "sometimes a dejected discouraged Christian thinks he hath so much to say against his comfort, as will put to silence the best and ablest Ministers."[27]

Let me risk one more anachronistic analogy. Consider the Puritans' paradoxical insight that knowledge can sometimes establish itself in the mind only when we give up trying to attain it. This is part of why Newman spoke of the inestimable worth of contemplation, and Whitman of loafing. The capacity for spiritual surprise, for apprehending without plan or foresight what Emerson called "the miraculous in the common" has been an enduring theme in psychological writing at least since Augustine, whose conversion, reported in the *Confessions*, comes upon him without volition, as a gift unsought and unearned.

In such cases, as Edwards wrote a millennium and a half later, "no improvement or composition of natural qualifications"—no effort, as we might say, to concentrate or focus—yields the desired result. Max Weber, a close student of the Protestant tradition to which Edwards belonged, put it this way: "ideas come when we do not expect them, and not when we are brooding and searching at our desks." We encounter the same point in Emerson's lecture on memory, in which he says that sometimes "we are assisted by a dream to recall what we could not find awake," and in Henry Adams's account of how his sullen indifference to the music of Beethoven suddenly gave way to an overwhelming sense of its hitherto unheard beauty:

> A prison-wall that barred his senses on one great side of life, suddenly fell, of its own accord, without so much as his knowing when it happened [and] a new sense burst out like a flower in his life, so superior to the old senses, so bewildering, so astonished at its own existence, that he could not credit it, and watched it as something apart, accidental, and not to be trusted.[28]

No effort or exertion precedes or leads to this breakthrough. It happens unbidden and in unlikely circumstances (amid the "fumes of coarse tobacco and poor beer" in a Berlin *rathskeller*), but it leaves the listener thoroughly and permanently transformed.

We may know more today than did Augustine, Edwards, Emerson, Weber, or Adams about the basic neurological processes that constitute memory or that account for the pleasure we take in creativity observed or expressed. Yet it is striking how little the latest theories of teaching and learning diverge from long-established views on these matters. Take, for example, William James on how one is sometimes blocked in the effort to retrieve an elusive memory:

> You know how it is when you try to recollect a forgotten name. Usually you help the recall by working for it, by mentally running over the places, persons, and things with which the word was connected. But sometimes this effort fails: you feel then as if the harder you tried the less hope there would be, as though the name were *jammed*, and pressure in its direction only kept it all the more from rising. And then the opposite expedient often succeeds. Give up the effort entirely; think of something altogether different, and in half an hour the lost name comes sauntering into your mind, as Emerson says, as carelessly as if it had never been invited. Some hidden process was started in you by the effort, which went on after the effort ceased, and made the result come as if it came spontaneously.[29]

Anyone who has ever stared at a math problem or struggled to write a recalcitrant sentence, and, after giving up, felt the elements fall into place with suddenly obvious ease, knows what James meant. Today, neuroscientists speak of the same phenomenon that he called jamming, but they are likely to use new acronyms such as TOTs ("Tip-of-the-Tongue events"), and come to the unsurprising conclusion that "massing"—or, to use the colloquial term, "cramming"—is a poor study method since exerting unremitting effort can defeat the purpose of the exertion.[30] On the basis of controlled experiment, they recommend that after asking a rhetorical question, a good teacher can get "generation benefits by leaving a pause before giving the answer"—in other words that "a mind must work to grow," and that students learn more by active thinking than by "passive absorption."[31] It's good to have data to corroborate these claims, but the most surprising thing about the findings is that they are presented as discoveries. The latter two phrases, "work to grow" and "passive absorption" are from 1869 (Charles W. Eliot) and 1915 (John Dewey). In 1870, Yale's clergyman president, Noah Porter, remarked that "the most effective teaching" is teaching by questioning—a pedagogical truth that has never been better demonstrated than in the Platonic dialogues composed some twenty-five hundred years ago.

4

In short, genuinely new educational ideas are rare. But sometimes old ones, such as the Socratic idea that learning is a collaborative rather than a solitary process, can take new form. That is what happened when the Christian idea of monastic community evolved into the idea of college as a place where students live as well as learn together. In this respect, too, the college idea, after it was carried to New England, echoed and extended the Puritans' conception of the church—by which they did not mean a physical structure of wood or stone (this they called the meetinghouse) but a voluntary gathering of seekers who come together for mutual support. Here is John Cotton on what constitutes a true church:

> I cannot tell how better to compare it than to a musical
> instrument, wherein though there be many pipes, yet one

blast of the bellowes puts breath into them all, so that all
of them at once break forth into a kind of melody, and
give a pleasant sound to the ears of those that stand by;
all of them do make but one Instrument, and one sound,
and yet variety of musick.[32]

In the relatively homogeneous society of colonial New England,
this aspiration toward unity in multiplicity—an early version,
one might say, of "*e pluribus unum*"—was doubtless more fanciful than actual. But as an ideal it was as basic to college as to the
church.

Cotton Mather invoked it when he noted in his history that
students in the university towns of continental Europe "board . . .
here and there at private houses," but that the English view, carried to New England, was that they should be "brought up in a
more *collegiate* way of living." College was about young people
from scattered origins converging to live together—taking their
meals together, attending lectures and sermons together, sharing
the daily rhythms of study and social life. At the heart of this
"collegiate way" was a concept of what might be called lateral
learning—the proposition that students have something important to learn from one another.[33]

This idea, routinely endorsed today in the websites and bro-
chures of many American colleges, has become so familiar that
we take it for granted. It is what Nathaniel Hawthorne (Bowdoin, class of 1825) had in mind when he remarked that "it con-
tributes greatly to a man's moral and intellectual health, to be
brought into habits of companionship with individuals unlike
himself, who care little for his pursuits, and whose sphere and
abilities he must go out of himself to appreciate." It is what Newman had in mind when he spoke of college as a place where stu-

dents are "brought, by familiar intercourse" into a relation where "they learn to respect, to consult, to aid each other." It's what Dewey meant when he described education as "a mode of social life" in which "the best and deepest moral training is precisely that which one gets through having to enter into proper relations with others in a unity of work and thought." It's why William Perry insisted that maturity in a college student means realizing there is something to learn from one's peers.[34]

The principle behind all these assertions may seem self-evident to us, but it is by no means universally so. With a few exceptions—such as Roosevelt Academy in the Netherlands (a branch of the University of Utrecht) or Lingnan University in Hong Kong—the residential college is virtually unknown outside the Anglo-American world. That is part of the point of Randall Jarrell's college novel *Pictures from an Institution* (1952) (a thinly veiled portrait of Bennington College), where émigré professors, grateful as they are to have found sanctuary from the Nazified universities of Europe, simply can't absorb the strange American notion that "students might be right about something" and the professor wrong.[35]

It is hard to overstate the importance of this idea of lateral learning. It is the source of the question that every admissions officer in every selective college is supposed to ask of every applicant: "what does this candidate bring to the class?" It underlies the opinion by Supreme Court Justice Lewis Powell in the "affirmative action" case of *Bakke vs. University of California* (1978), in which the court ruled that consideration of a candidate's race is constitutional for the purpose of ensuring "the interplay of ideas and the exchange of views" among students from different backgrounds. These are modern reformulations of the ancient (by American standards) view that a college, no less than a church, exists fundamentally as an "interaction of consciences," and that admission should be based primarily on the candidate's "aptness to edifie another."[36]

5

The place where the idea comes alive, or at least where it can and should, is the classroom. Here is an account of what the idea in practice meant for one student, born and schooled in China, who came to the United States not long ago in order to attend Bowdoin (founded 1794), where he encountered the modern version of the Puritan principle that no communicant should "take any ancient doctrine for truth till they have examined it" for themselves:

> Coming from a culture in which a "standard answer" is provided for every question, I did not argue with others even when I disagreed. However, Bowdoin forced me to re-consider "the answer" and reach beyond my comfort zone. In my first-year seminar, "East Asian Politics," I was required to debate with others and develop a habit of class engagement. This sometimes meant raising coun- terarguments or even disagreeing with what had been put forward. For instance, one day we debated what roles Confucianism played in the development of Chinese democracy. Of the 16 students in the classroom, 15 agreed that Confucianism impeded China's development; but I disagreed. I challenged my classmates. Bowdoin made me consistently question the "prescribed answer." That was the biggest challenge for me.[37]

A necessary, though not sufficient, condition for this kind of learning is small class size—which is why, in all but the very richest institutions, educational and fiscal interests are always in tension. The educational premise is simple: a class should be small enough to permit every student to participate in the give-and-take of discussion. The economics are simple too: the lower the ratio between students and faculty (especially tenured faculty), the higher the cost.

Yet in many colleges the principle is defended with impressive ferocity, especially by alumni who want future students to have something like the experience they had, and who make generous contributions to that end. I have seen it at work in an array of institutions, at public colleges such as the Beaufort branch of the University of South Carolina, or Norwalk Community College in coastal Connecticut, as well as at colleges in what is sometimes called the American "heartland"—some of them keenly aware of their Protestant (if not strictly Puritan) heritage, such as Valparaiso University in Indiana, Wheaton College in Illinois, Baylor University in Texas, Geneva College in western Pennsylvania, to name just a few. Of course, the institutional and individual descendants of the people who invented the idea of lateral learning exercise no monopoly over it. It is not a Puritan idea, or a Protestant idea; it is a timeless idea—as evident in Talmudic debate or Socratic dialogue as in the Anglo-American college. But in the context of such a college it presents certain distinctive problems and possibilities.

A renowned teacher at my own institution, Lionel Trilling, remarked near the end of his life that when, "through luck or cunning," small-group discussion works well, it "can have special pedagogic value." Coming from Trilling, whose quietly reflective style gave him great intensity in the classroom (students called him, with no irony intended, "Thrilling Trilling"), this was high praise. What he meant was that a small class can help students learn how to qualify their initial responses to hard questions. It can help them learn the difference between informed insights and mere opinionating. It can provide the pleasurable chastisement of discovering that others see the world differently, and that their experience is not replicable by, or even reconcilable with, one's own. At its best, a small class is an exercise in deliberative democracy, in which the teacher is neither oracle nor lawgiver but a kind of provocateur.

Let me offer an example from my own experience. It was a literature class in which the students also happened to be teachers themselves—high school teachers from a public school in central North Carolina. One of the poems we read together was a well-known poem by Emily Dickinson, of which these are the first two stanzas:

> My Life had stood—a Loaded Gun—
> In Corners—till a Day
> The Owner passed—identified—
> And carried Me away—
>
> And now We roam in Sovereign Woods—
> And now We hunt the Doe—
> And every time I speak for Him—
> The Mountains straight reply—

This poem may be read as a woman's account of how it feels to be confined to the status of an instrument of a man's will, allowed only enough independence to serve as a facilitator of his pleasure. At first, the students seemed convinced by such a reading, and they added to the discussion many particular insights that tended to support it.

Then, toward the end of the session, as we were considering the later stanzas ("And do I smile, such cordial light / Upon the Valley glow — / It is as a Vesuvian face / Had let its pleasure through —"), one usually voluble member of the class, who had been strikingly silent, spoke up. What she said was roughly this: this poem moves me as an expression of erotic power. It reads like a transcript of my own marriage ("And when at Night — Our good Day done — / I guard My Master's Head — / 'Tis better than the Eider-Duck's / Deep Pillow — to have shared —"). It celebrates the completion of one human life by its cleaving to another. It is a love poem about how surrendering the will can enlarge the self. What we concluded at the end of our discussion was not that one side or the other had won the day on behalf of its preferred reading, but that the poem existed in the difference between them.

I can think of many such occasions when a student's intervention broke up a complacent consensus in my class. And yet small classes hardly guarantee large learning. "There will be students," as Trilling went on to say, "who cannot be induced to say anything at all, and there will be those who cannot be kept from trying to say everything." And, he added, "even a measured articulateness does not ensure the cogency of what is said."

This remark puts me in mind of a story our son told my wife and me some years ago on a visit home from college. He was taking an art history course, and the discussion leader, a graduate student teaching for the first time, projected onto the screen a slide reproduction of Alfred Stieglitz's famous photograph "The Steerage," showing emigrants packed onto the deck of a ship in New York harbor. One of the students, very bright and self-assured, launched into a discussion of the "liminality" of the voyagers, as conveyed by the blurry quality of the image; the journey, she said, had half-erased them, leeching out of them their

Old World identity before they had formed a new identity in the New World. Other students developed the point, contributing competitive allusions to various theories of "hegemony" and "alterity" until one student suggested that the teacher try adjusting the slide projector. Sure enough, the image came sharply into focus—but the discussion went on undeterred. The moral of the story (of special salience to the humanities these days) is that it's always a good idea to bring one's bullshit meter to class, and to expect that now and then the needle will jump off the dial.

And yet a well-managed discussion can be of exceptional effect. It can envelop the mind in multiple perspectives that lead toward what William James (a great teacher to whom W.E.B. DuBois looked as "my guide to clear thinking") called "that ideal vanishing-point towards which we imagine that all our temporary truths will some day converge."[38] That phrase captures a distinctively American conception of truth as always in flux, in-the-making rather than ready-made. This pragmatist conception of truth runs counter to the idea of revelation received and absorbed by persons who have nothing to add to it except their consent. In that sense, it is an idea at odds with the "Augustinian strain of piety" that animated the Puritan mind and out of which several of our first colleges took form. But Puritanism also had within it a proto-democratic conception of truth emerging through discussion and debate among human beings who are inherently equal.

6

There was another form of teaching toward which the founders of the first American colleges felt particular devotion. This was the lecture—originally a medieval term (derived from the Latin *legere*, to read) for reading aloud and explicating scriptural, patristic, or classical texts by scholars whose students, in the pre-Gutenberg era, rarely possessed books of their own. In the Puritan tradition, the word "lecture" acquired a more specific meaning. By the later sixteenth century, in parishes where the resident clergyman was unable or unwilling to satisfy the public demand for preaching, unsatisfied laity sometimes hired supplementary lecturers, typically men fresh out of college, whose charge was to preach several times each week—on weekdays as well as on the Sabbath.

Committed as they were to what I have called lateral learning, Puritans nevertheless suspected that too much talk from the laity with too little guidance from the clergy could lead to insolence and heresy—and so they stressed the need to hear from learned lecturers as well as from themselves. In fact, their zeal for sermons became a point of sore dispute in old England, where the state church emphasized the sonic and scenic aspects of public worship—the sound of the organ, the sight of the scarlet-clad priest seen in light refracted through stained glass. For those who took seriously St. Paul's injunction that "faith cometh by hearing" (Romans 10:17), this kind of spectacle was both too little and too much. One reason they emigrated to New England in the first place was their belief that the infusion of grace was likeliest to occur not while a penitent sinner was witnessing the sacraments or even while taking communion, but when he or she was listening to a gospel preacher whose voice could melt the heart.

The ideal listener was inwardly restless, measuring the preacher's claims against his own experience ("Go home and consider whether the things that have been taught were true or no," John Cotton told his listeners), searching her mind for scriptural analogues to what he or she was feeling.[39] Although a lecture takes place in public, listening to it was—and, ideally, still is—a fundamentally private experience. "The preacher's words had taken a deep impression on my conscience," one young Englishman reported in his diary around 1590, yet the same words made so little impression on his friends that they "fell upon me in jesting manner," full of mockery and contempt.[40] Puritans were so committed to this half-private, half-public form of religious experience, and so convinced that the lecture-sermon was among God's ways of sorting the saved from the damned, that in early New England, to which one faction removed in order to found sermon-drenched churches, the average churchgoer could expect to attend roughly seven thousand sermons in a lifetime, which amounted (since a sermon might last two hours or more) to nearly "fifteen thousand hours of concentrated listening."[41]

This was the context—a world saturated by the spoken word—in which the American college first arose, and from which the modern college lecture derives. Scientists have believed in it as strongly as those whom today we would call humanists. Two centuries after the founding of Harvard, we find William Barton Rogers, a professor of chemistry at William and Mary and the University of Virginia, who went on to become the first president of MIT, unfavorably comparing "exclusive textbook study and recitation" to the "greater impressiveness of knowledge *orally* conveyed."[42] The tradition that Rogers invoked was not, as we might think, that of the thundering preacher who sends forth settled TRUTH from his pulpit or podium. There were, no doubt, such preacher-teachers, and always will be. But the real power of the tradition lies in its exploratory reflectiveness, as when the teacher speaks from sketchy notes rather than from a controlling script, in order to allow spontaneous self-revision. He or she speaks from inside the subject, with an openness to new discoveries even while moving through an argument made many times before. No good lecture (or sermon) should be closed to second thoughts; it must have a dialogic quality—a spirit of self-questioning that draws the listeners into honest inquiry into themselves.

But what should we make today of this time-honored trust in the power of the spoken word? In our wired world, it is hard to imagine sitting for hours in a drafty meetinghouse silent except for the sound of the preaching voice, pinned to one's pew by the eyes of a clergyman who seems somehow privy to one's secret sins. Some educators today think that the college lecture has become as obsolete as the hellfire sermon. Rather than listening continuously, many students are e-mailing, texting, and checking their "smart" phones during class. As for those who do unplug themselves for a while, what, exactly, are they supposed to get from a long monologue when they are accustomed to surfing and multitasking and "dealing with multiple information streams in short bursts"? It's a question that goes to the larger question of whether America's colleges can still lay claim to a useable past.

At least the beginning of an answer is suggested by Emerson's comment that "it is not instruction, but provocation, that I can receive from another soul." The hallmark of the great lecturer has always been the power to provoke, and there is no reason to think this power diminished. In fact, in our age of degraded public speech, such a lecturer fills a need—if not, to use today's ubiquitous marketing language, a niche. One lecturer may be hotly demonstrative, another so shyly inattentive to the students in the room that they feel they have eavesdropped on a private conversation between the speaker and herself. I still hear from Columbia alumni of a certain age how they flocked to listen to Meyer Schapiro, the great art historian whose glowing eyes and transported smile as he spoke of Cézanne or Kandinsky led more than one student to say, "Whatever he's smoking, I'll have some."

Or consider this account of William James by another grateful student, George Santayana:

> Perhaps in the first years of his teaching he felt a little in the professor's chair as a military man might feel when obliged to read the prayers at a funeral. He probably conceived what he said more deeply than a more scholastic mind might have conceived it; yet he would have been more comfortable if someone else had said it for him. He liked to open the window, and look out for a moment. I think he was glad when the bell rang, and he could be himself again until the next day. But in the midst of this routine of the class-room the spirit would sometimes come upon him, and, leaning his head on his hand, he would let fall golden words, picturesque, fresh from the heart, full of the knowledge of good and evil.[43]

In this passage we get not only a portrait of a great teacher but a glimpse of what college at its best can be.

7

To anyone even glancingly acquainted with the history of American education, it is hardly news that our colleges have their origins in religion, or that they derive their aims, structure, and pedagogical methods mainly from Protestantism, and, more particularly, from the stringent form of Protestantism whose partisans were called—at first derisively by their enemies, later proudly by themselves—Puritans. Many colleges, both old and relatively new, retain vestiges of their religious origins in, for example, the neo-Gothic architecture of the library or in a chapel spire that rises above the center (or what was once the center) of campus and from which everything else radiates outward.

Yet many academics have a curiously uneasy relation with these origins, as if they pose some threat or embarrassment to our secular liberties, even though the battle for academic freedom against clerical authority was won long ago. If you were to remind just about any major university president today that his or her own institution arose from this or that religious denomination, you'd likely get the response of the proverbial Victorian lady who, upon hearing of Darwin's claim that men descend from apes, replied that she hoped it wasn't so—but if it were, that it not become widely known.

This is a pity and a waste, since there is much to be learned from the past, including the clerical past, about the essential aims and challenges of college education. We tend not to remember, or perhaps half-deliberately to forget, that college was once conceived not as a road to wealth or as a screening service for a social club, but as a training ground for pastors, teachers, and, more broadly, public servants. Founded as philanthropic institutions, the English originals of America's colleges were "expected," as Morison put it, "to dispense alms to outsiders, as well as charity to their own children."[44] Benjamin Franklin, founder of the University of Pennsylvania, who was both a conservator and renovator of the Puritan tradition, put it this way: "The idea of what is *true merit*, should . . . be often presented to youth, explain'd and impress'd on their minds, as consisting in an *Inclination* join'd with an *Ability* to serve Mankind, one's Country, Friends, and Family . . . which Ability should be the great *Aim* and *End* of all learning."[45]

Franklin's friend Benjamin Rush founded Dickinson College a hundred miles west of Philadelphia, in Carlisle, Pennsylvania, with the stipulation that it be built near the courthouse—so that its students, as Dickinson's current president puts it, could make the short walk to "observe government in action" and become "engaged with their society in order to prepare them to lead in it."[46] In our own time, when some colleges seem to have less than a firm grasp on their public obligations, such precedents—from both the era of religion and of Enlightenment—should not be cause for embarrassment but for emulation.

As for obligations to our "own children"—to students, that is— it may help to recall the derivation of the word by which we name the person who stands at the lectern or sits at the head of the seminar table. That word, of course, is "professor"—a term that once referred to a person who professes a faith, as in the Puritan churches, where the profession was made before the congregation as a kind of public initiation. Surely this meaning is one to which we should still wish to lay claim, since the true teacher must always be a professor in the root sense of the word—a person undaunted by the incremental fatigue of repetitive work, who remains ardent, even fanatic, in the service of his calling.

THREE

FROM COLLEGE TO UNIVERSITY

Nearly a century after the first English settlement at Jamestown, and eighty years after the "pilgrims" landed at Plymouth, there were still only two colleges in the American colonies, Harvard (founded in 1636) in the north, and William and Mary (1693) in the upper south. Between the outset of the eighteenth century and the outbreak of the Revolution, the number grew to nine, with New England, New York, New Jersey, and Pennsylvania accounting for all the growth. The two oldest colleges were joined by Yale (1701); The College of New Jersey (1746), which became Princeton University in 1896; King's College (1754), which took a patriotic new name, Columbia, in 1784; the College of Philadelphia (chartered in 1755, it became the University of Pennsylvania in 1779); the College in the Colony of Rhode Island and Providence Plantations (1764), renamed in 1804 for an early benefactor, Nicholas Brown; Queen's College (1766), which became Rutgers in 1825, in honor of a Revolutionary War hero; and Dartmouth (1769), which began in 1754, in Connecticut, as a missionary school for Indians, before obtaining its college charter and moving to its present location in Hanover, New Hampshire.[1]

In some cases, new colleges arose for reasons similar to those that drove proliferation of the churches: one faction, out of disaffection with its brethren, or because of the inconvenience or expense of travel, broke away and formed a new congregation in a new neighborhood. Thus Yale was founded in part because Cotton Mather, a member of Harvard's governing board, became so unhappy with the fall from orthodoxy in Cambridge that he encouraged the formation of a new college a hundred miles south, at New Haven, that would cleave more closely to the faith.

Yale, in turn, provided impetus for a new institution yet further south when a hotly pious student, David Brainerd, accused his tutor during the Great Awakening of the 1740s of having "no more grace than the chair I am leaning on" and got himself kicked out for his impudence. When sympathetic "New Light" alumni, including Jonathan Edwards and Aaron Burr (father of the future vice president and dueling opponent of Alexander Hamilton), concluded that Yale, no less than Harvard, had gone hopelessly cold, they gave their support to a new college at "Prince-Town"— about which Burr was later supposed to have said, "if it had not been for the treatment received by Mr. Brainerd at Yale College, New Jersey College would never have been erected."[2] A more secular version of the same schismatic process led Thomas Jefferson, early in the nineteenth century, to found the University of Virginia as a corrective to the "languor and inefficiency" into which his alma mater, William and Mary, had fallen.[3]

By the 1820s, the pace was accelerating at which new colleges were forming—again, in some instances, by disgruntled refugees from older ones, as when Oberlin (founded in 1833) opened its doors to students and faculty from nearby Lane Theological

Seminary, who had become enraged at the Lane administration for suppressing debate over slavery. By now the United States had some fifty colleges, though relative to the whole population their total enrollment was still tiny—fewer than four thousand students out of thirteen million people. Some were short-lived, others were to become eminent and enduring, and most remained closely allied with this or that denomination—so much so, as one Yale graduate complained in 1852, that "you go sixteen times a week to chapel, or woe to you."[4]

Endowments were generally meager, tuition revenue dependent on unpredictable enrollments (students typically numbered between thirty and a hundred), and support from the local denomination variable. In the words of historian Richard Hofstadter, most colleges were "precarious little institutions, denomination-ridden, poverty-stricken . . . in fact not colleges at all, but glorified high schools or academies that presumed to offer degrees."[5] In a lively recent book, the writer Anya Kamenetz puts it more pungently: "any college that trumpets its 'centuries-long tradition of academic excellence' is lying."[6]

Such, at least, was once the standard account of so-called higher education before the Civil War—that it amounted to a smattering of weak institutions of little use to young men entering the labor market or the still-small managerial class. It is not hard to find contemporaries who buttress this view. In *Moby-Dick* (1851), when the owner of the whale ship *Pequod* wants to convey to young Ishmael that he is shipping out under a strange (to put it mildly) captain, he tells the boy that Captain Ahab "has been in colleges as well as among the cannibals," as if only a very peculiar person would venture into the vicinity of either. Future senator Charles Sumner (Harvard, class of 1830) remarked that "*not one single thing* is well taught to the Undergraduates of

Harvard College." Henry Adams (class of 1858), concurred that the college "taught little, and that little ill" and sent him into the world as "an autobiographical blank."[7] For many students, college was a deadening routine of memorization and "recitation" whereby you stood before your professor to demonstrate your mastery, or to expose your deficiency, at scanning Horace or Virgil, or performing a mathematical calculation, or finding the right scriptural passage with which to justify a theological point.

And if work was dull, discipline—at least so it seemed to outsiders—was nil. According to one member of the Peabody family, crimes "worthy of the penitentiary were of frequent occurrence" in the New England colleges, including setting off explosives, smashing windows, stoning the homes of unpopular faculty members, stealing chickens, "borrowing" horses and returning them with manes shorn. That perennial form of student protest—the food riot—was so common that college seemed little more than a "disorderly burlesque." One student in Virginia, expelled for inciting a hissing protest at supper against what he called "fly-soup," did not make clear whether he thought the soup had been concocted of boiled flies or the hall was so infested that too many flies drowned in his bowl. Either way, his classmates joined him in loud solidarity.[8]

Crediting this image of college as stultifying and joyless unless students took matters into their own hands, some accounts render these years as what used to be called, by historians of medieval Europe, the "dark ages." In fact, many books about higher education, to the extent that they consider a sense of the past useful at all for understanding the present, begin the story after the Civil War with the rise of the research university and ignore the putatively primitive "old-time college" altogether.[9] There is doubtless something right about that version, but there is also a good deal wrong with—or at least missing from—it. It is rather like dismissing those who lived before us because they did not live in houses with central heating or because they held retrograde views about race or religion or sex.

In fact, a number of experiments in educational reform were under way by the 1820s and '30s, and many colleges were lively sites of debate about religion and politics as well as education itself. The new University of Virginia offered what today we would call eight "tracks"—including in specialized subjects such as anatomy and law. At a number of relatively young colleges, including Union (1795), Amherst (1821), Hobart (founded as Geneva College in 1822), and Trinity (founded as Washington College in 1823), modern languages and science began to supplant the classics—and the rumblings of reform were felt, too, at venerable institutions such as Harvard and Yale.[10]

The fact is that something of value was happening in the colleges regardless of where they stood on the curricular debates—or at least some students were bringing something valuable with them to college. The Civil War historian James McPherson points out, for example, the extraordinarily high percentage of college graduates among leaders of the abolitionist movement. In a sample of 250 antislavery leaders, nearly 80 percent had either been graduated from, or spent some time in, a college—and this at a period when less than 2 percent of the overall population was college educated.[11] But did this mean that going to college had something to do with acquiring, or at least heightening, a sense of outrage at slavery? Or did it mean that young men with "knives in their brains" (Emerson's phrase for the youth of the 1830s) ready for carving up assumptions held dear by their elders were more likely to go to college than those with dull minds and a tendency to acquiesce?

This sort of question—the chicken-and-egg sort, or what is sometimes called the question of cause versus correlation—is impossible to answer with much confidence, especially when asked of the past. Were colleges enlarging the minds of their students? Or were those who went to college more likely than others to be large-minded before they got there? The evidence pushes in opposite directions. On the one hand, to stay for a moment with the case of race, between 1826 and 1866 a total of twenty-eight African Americans in the entire United States received bachelor's degrees out of a black population that, by the end of that period, exceeded four and a half million, including more than six hundred thousand emancipated before the Civil War, some whose families had been free for generations.[12] On the other hand, some colleges clearly attracted young citizens with reform on their minds—not only new colleges such as Oberlin, the first to be genuinely integrated as well as the first committed to coeducation, but also old ones. On an American book tour in 1842, Charles Dickens found the United States to be a vulgar country driven by the democratically distributed motive of greed, but he made an exception for the "University of Cambridge" (his name for the same Harvard that Sumner and Adams disparaged), which he praised for "the humanising tastes and desires it has engendered; the affectionate friendships to which it has given rise; the amount of vanity and prejudice it has dispelled."[13]

No doubt some antebellum colleges were regressive, stuffy, and mired in the past. Others were restless, open, and vibrant. At least through the mid-1800s, most retained some version of the religious uniformity with which they had begun (Princeton was Presbyterian, Brown was Baptist, and so on), but whatever their particular creed in what has been aptly called "an age of moral pedagogy," they agreed that their primary purpose remained the development of sound character in their students.

To that end, a senior-year course in moral philosophy, taught by the college president, was virtually universal, though details varied from college to college according to its particular religious affiliation. As one historian describes it, the course (today we would call it the "capstone experience") was "designed to draw together all the scrambled admonitions and reprimands that had theretofore been lavished on a youth, to arrange them in a systematic body, and offer them as the moral legacy of the ages to be studied, cherished, and presumably, obeyed throughout life."[14]

The view of human character thus systematized was not very different in its essentials from that of the Puritan founders, though there now tended to be more allowance for willed self-improvement and less emphasis on seizure of the soul by irresistible grace. Here, as expounded by James McCosh, a Scottish-born philosopher in the tradition of John Witherspoon, another Scotsman, who had preceded him as president of Princeton, is a representative statement:

> Freedom and law are . . . the fundamental charters of
> [the] kingdom of mind. The mind is virtuous when the
> two are in union, when the free will is moving in accor-
> dance with the fixed law. The mind is criminal when the
> free will is unfaithful to her partner and husband the law.
> There begin from that instant that schism, those family
> dissensions, if we so speak, which do so distract the soul.
> And from these inward contests there can be no escape
> by means of a lawful divorce. . . . Hence that internal
> dissension which rages in the breasts of all whose will has
> rebelled against the law of their nature, that is, the law of

God—a schism which, but for Divine interposition, must
exist for ever, it being impossible for the distracted parties
either to separate on the one hand, or cordially to unite
on the other.[15]

Going to college was an exercise in self-examination, self-discipline,
and self-abnegation. Or so, at least, it was supposed to be.

2

But if Puritanism retained residual force in the doctrinaire religion taught in the nineteenth-century college, those who did
the teaching felt under increasing pressure to prove the worth of
their work. By the second half of the century, a defensive tone was
creeping into the official communications that all colleges issue—
now as then—to appeal for public support. We find Yale's president, for example, in a book tellingly titled *The American Colleges and the American Public* (1870), extolling college life with a
lengthy catalogue of benefits that suggests a certain anxiety in his
salesmanship: "the warmth of college friendships, the earnestness
of college rivalries, the revelations of character, the manifestations
of growth, the issues of villainy and passion in retribution and
shame, the rewards of perseverance in triumph and honor . . ."[16]
Points that would once have gone without saying—the value of
Christian education, of training in the Greek and Latin classics,
of living at close quarters with one's peers—were now proclaimed
by colleges defending themselves against public doubt.

In some quarters, doubt turned to derision. By the early 1890s,
the largely self-educated Andrew Carnegie was denouncing "college education as it exists today," with its focus on antiquated ideas
and "dead languages," as suitable only "for life on another planet."[17]
A few years later, the Irish-born Chicago journalist Finley Peter

Dunne, writing in the voice of the fictional Mr. Dooley, identified two types of college: the "Colledge iv Speechless Thought" and "th' Colledge iv Thoughtless Speech." In the latter,

> Th' head iv this colledge believes in thrainin' young
> men f'r th' civic ideel. . . . He believes 'young men shud
> be equipped with Courage, Discipline, an' Loftiness iv
> Purpose;' so I suppose Packy [Dooley's son], if he wint
> there, wud listen to lectures fr'm . . . Erasmus H. Noddle,
> Doctor iv Loftiness iv Purpose. I loft, ye loft, he lofts. I've
> always felt we needed some wan to teach our young th'
> Courage they can't get walkin' home in th' dark, an' th'
> loftiness iv purpose that doesn't start with bein' hungry
> an' lookin' f'r wurruk. An' in th' colledge where these
> studies are taught, its undhershtud that even betther thin
> gettin' th' civic ideel is bein' head iv a thrust.[18]

Some thirty years later, in *Horsefeathers* (1932), Groucho Marx weighed in as President Quincy Adams Wagstaff, of Huxley U., who breaks out into a spontaneous song of himself:

> I don't know what they have to say / It makes no differ-
> ence anyway / Whatever it is, I'm against it. / No matter
> what it is or who commenced it, I'm against it! / Your
> proposition may be good / But let's have one thing under-
> stood: / Whatever it is, I'm against it. / And even when
> you've changed it or condensed it, I'm against it! / For
> months before my son was born / I used to yell from night
> till morn: / Whatever it is, I'm against it! / And I've kept
> yelling since I've first commenced it, I'm against it.

As long as colleges remained securely connected to mainstream American culture, this kind of thing could be shrugged off as just so much grousing by people left outside the campus gates. But by Dunne's time, and long before Groucho's, the connection was becoming strained.

The strain had many causes. One obvious problem for the old-time colleges was their resolute Protestantism in a society of increasing religious and ethnic diversity (the few Catholic institutions, beginning with Georgetown, founded in 1789, were initially seminaries for aspirants to the priesthood). In 1850, more than nine out of ten Americans had been born in the United States; by the centennial year of 1876, more Americans were foreign-born than would be the case a hundred years later.[19] Another problem was the publication, in 1859, of Darwin's *The Origin of Species*, whose enervating effect on religious orthodoxy had been anticipated as early as the 1830s by geologists who estimated the age of the earth to be much older than what the Bible seemed to warrant, as well as by advocates of a "higher criticism" who questioned the divine authorship of the Bible itself.

The story of how theology lost its primacy, and how nature, history, and human psychology came increasingly to be viewed from a scientific rather than a religious perspective has been told in many variations by many historians. Darwin is a convenient starting point, but in truth the story has no distinct beginning or—since we are still in the midst of it—clear end. For our purposes, it may be enough to say that the transformation of the colleges, as of everything else in American life, became evidently imperative in the aftermath of the Civil War, which opened, to use Emerson's geologic metaphor, "a cleavage in the hitherto granite of the past."[20]

Not a few colleges fell into that chasm (for one thing, the war drained students away for military service), some never emerged, and those that did survive found themselves in a nation vastly expanded by westward settlement and immigration but also contracted by new networks of communication (first the telegraph, then the telephone) and transport (the railroads, later the automobile), and with a pressing need for expert training in modern industrial, agricultural, bureaucratic, and legal techniques.[21] Even before the midpoint of the war, Congress passed the Morrill Act (1862) providing grants of federal land to the loyal states—thirty thousand acres for each of its senators and representatives—earmarked for the purpose of establishing new colleges "where the leading object shall be, without excluding other scientific or classical studies, to teach such branches of learning as are related to agriculture and the mechanic arts." These "land-grant" colleges eventually evolved into the system of state universities that today includes such institutions of international caliber as the University of Illinois, Pennsylvania State University, and many more.

At the same time, the old apprenticeship system was shrinking, and careers such as law and medicine were beginning to require a professional degree both as evidence of competence and as a device for gatekeeping. To prepare young men for modern careers, colleges began to move beyond prescribed curricula centered on theology and the classics. Every college, in every era, tries to accommodate its felt obligations to the past (represented by alumni and veteran faculty), the present (boards of trustees, legislatures, current donors), and the future (new and prospective students)—and the nineteenth-century college was no exception. With or without the consent of all its constituents, the pace of change, begun in the antebellum years, accelerated. The number of elective courses in specialized subjects multiplied, students were assigned to recitation sections according to their proficiency as demonstrated by examination or by passing a prerequisite course, and instruction was increasingly organized through academic departments rather than controlled by the president or a coterie of faculty elders.[22]

It is tempting to construe such changes as a sudden and total break from the past—an onslaught by modernity on what had been essentially a premodern conception of what education should be. In fact, long before Darwin or the Civil War or the ensuing intellectual, social, and economic transformations, there had been notable dissenters who saw America's colleges as hopelessly backward and irrelevant to what was needed. As early as the 1730s, Benjamin Franklin was lampooning Harvard as an intellectually constipated place, and he soon suggested a new kind of college at Philadelphia (it eventually became the University of Pennsylvania) that would produce "discoveries . . . to the benefit of mankind." Franklin's fellow Philadelphian Benjamin Rush envisioned a great university that would be an incubator of American progress, and, during his presidency (1808–1816), James Madison proposed a federally funded university—to no avail—in no fewer than four messages to Congress.

When research universities finally did emerge in the post–Civil War years, the colleges—even those that did not become universities themselves—had no choice but to adapt to them. The very word "university" acquired a new meaning. It had previously been used interchangeably with the word "college," but now it denoted an entirely different kind of institution whose mission encompassed research and professional training alongside the teaching of "undergraduates"—a term that came into general use in order to distinguish candidates for the college degree from those pursuing more advanced studies. Some of the new universities took shape around the core of a colonial college (Harvard, Yale, Columbia), while others, such as Chicago and Northwestern, came into being without any preexisting foundation and with initial benefactions from such captains of industry as Carnegie and John D. Rockefeller. Still others (Clark, Johns Hopkins) were founded with no undergraduate students at all.

On the Columbia campus, which was mainly built in the first decade of the twentieth century after the university had moved uptown in order to make room for its growing research activities, there stands a domed building with these words inscribed across its façade: *"Erected for the Students that Religion and Learning May Go Hand in Hand and Character Grow with Knowledge."* Whenever I walk past this building, which still houses the office of the campus chaplain, I think of a point that one of my teachers insisted upon as an axiom of intellectual history: when a principle is explicitly expressed in formal proclamations or monuments, it's a good bet that contemporaries no longer believe it. "Erected for the students" suggests that the other university buildings were erected for something else. And so they were: for advancing a particular discipline such as mathematics or chemistry or law. As for religion, it was becoming an anachronism, and was certainly no longer at the center of campus life.

All the rising American universities—whether new or renewed—were modeled to one degree or another on the renowned German universities of the day, where academic freedom prevailed, research laboratories as well as graduate seminars first attained their modern form, and "professors could function exclusively as scholars and researchers" since they "did not have to bother themselves with remedying undergraduate deficiencies."[23] In due course, these emerging institutions absorbed schools of medicine and law that had begun independently, and acquired teacher-training schools, along with schools of engineering and business.

One aspect of the new universities was the transformation of their faculties into certified professionals, complete with a peer review system and national standards for accreditation. In effect, regulatory authority over higher education shifted from the churches to such academic associations as the Modern Language Association (founded in 1883), the American Historical Association (1884), and the American Mathematical Society (1888)—a process that culminated in 1915 with the formation of the American Association of University Professors (AAUP) under the leadership of John Dewey and Arthur Lovejoy, a distinguished historian at Johns Hopkins, for the purpose of defending academic freedom from incursions by presidents and trustees. Sporadic conflict between faculties and presidents persisted into the twentieth century, as when Charles Beard, Columbia's leading historian, resigned in 1917 over the firing by President Nicholas Murray Butler of two faculty members who had publicly opposed America's engagement in World War I. (Beard described the university trustees who stood with Butler as "reactionary and visionless in politics, narrow and medieval in religion.") But on a national scale the tide had turned. In 1895, Andrew Dickson White, first president of Cornell, whose private endowment was augmented by land granted to New York State under the Morrill Act, looked back at the era of the old denominational colleges and declared himself well rid of "a system of control which, in selecting a Professor of Mathematics or Language or Rhetoric or Physics or Chemistry, asked first and above all to what sect or even to what wing or branch of a sect he belonged."[24]

By the end of the nineteenth century the American college found itself in an utterly transformed environment, of which the most conspicuous institutional feature was the new university. In its orientation toward specialized scholarship and research, the university was both a rival to the colleges and—as the PhD degree became the standard credential for college teaching (by

1903, William James was warning against "the PhD octopus")—
the source of future faculty even for those colleges that remained
apart from the new universities. This was both a boon and a
problem. It encouraged professionalism and elevated standards
throughout American higher education. But it also created a
context in which ambitious academics regarded teaching undergraduates as a distraction and a burden.

At universities that had taken form around an established
college, proposals were floated to relegate undergraduate teaching to what amounted to a second-class faculty of failed or former researchers, while at some urban institutions there were even
plans to ship undergraduates out from the main campus to some
affiliated college in the country.[25] In the view of William Rainey
Harper, first president of the University of Chicago, keeping college students around at all was "a temporary concession to the
weakness of the founder" (John D. Rockefeller), who, inexplica-
bly, had a soft spot for them.[26] Meanwhile, faculty began to benefit from competitive recruitments. And when a rival university
came wooing, one of the first things to bargain for was a reduced
teaching load in order to free up time for research—as when the
Harvard philologist Francis James Child was excused, in 1876,
from grading undergraduate papers in response to a job offer
from Johns Hopkins.[27]

In retrospect it all seems a predestined process that led inexo-
rably to the educational hierarchy we take for granted today, in
which the word "college" has been reduced from an honorific de-
noting high educational attainment to a kind of diminutive—a
baby step in the credentialing process. It's now been forty years
since the Carnegie Commission on Higher Education established formal classifications by which to rank institutions in this
hierarchy, with universities ("research" and "comprehensive")

at the top, and colleges ("liberal arts," "community") at the bottom. This naming system has yet to take into account the explosive growth of for-profit institutions, which defy classification, though at least one critic thinks they deserve a category all their own: "marketing machines masquerading as universities."[28]

One effect of the formalized hierarchy, as the Carnegie Foundation (parent organization of the commission) has lately recognized, is that "many institutions have sought to 'move up' the classification system."[29] Some institutions that are essentially liberal arts colleges, such as Wesleyan, Drew, or the University of the South (better known as Sewanee), call themselves universities on the grounds that they enroll a relatively few graduate students. In short, academic culture today regards the research university as the most evolved species in the institutional chain of being, and implies—or at least invites the inference—that those below it exhibit varying degrees of truncation or failure. This process of invidious differentiation began in the second half of the nineteenth century, when, as one historian puts it, America's colleges were first "bitten by the bug of university aspiration."[30]

3

One way to follow the process is to pay attention to the internal debates that broke out within and between those colleges that were in the best position to become universities—as when Princeton's McCosh and Harvard's Eliot met on neutral ground in New York in 1885 to discuss what a college curriculum should be. McCosh came to defend what he called the "Trinity of studies"—"Language and Literature . . . Science, and . . . Philosophy"—which, under his first and third rubrics, still included Classics. Though he was certainly the more conservative of the two presidents, he was not the hidebound traditionalist that detractors made him out to be. In fact, soon after arriving at Princeton in 1868, he had introduced elective courses (to the dismay of some faculty), although the range of choice was strictly limited, and only juniors and seniors could choose them while freshmen and sophomores continued to follow a fully prescribed curriculum. McCosh believed that "physical science" should be included in every course of study, but he also insisted that "mental and moral science" must be required of all students. This was because impressionable young people are susceptible to the temptation of unbelief: if "our students are instructed only in matter they are apt to conclude there is nothing but matter."[31]

Eliot, on the other hand, was convinced that "a well-instructed youth of eighteen can select for himself a better course of study than any college faculty." Several premises underlay this view: that a good college does a good job of choosing worthy students capable of self-direction, that individual differences in talent and disposition should be cultivated and encouraged, and that the college atmosphere of healthy competition will ensure the student's will to excel in whatever field seems most congenial and absorbing. Besides, "at eighteen the American boy has passed the age when a compulsory external discipline is useful."[32] In short, McCosh was for control and guidance, while Eliot was for freedom.

Behind their disagreement were two very different views of the psychological and intellectual development of young men. Eliot believed that the internalization of responsible ambition occurs before college if it is to occur at all. McCosh considered such early maturity unlikely or at least unreliable. In this respect his judgment was either informed or—depending on one's view of it—distorted, by his wide acquaintance with educational institutions not only in Scotland and England, but in Germany, Switzerland, and Holland. In general, he was right that the graduates of European equivalents of America's high schools (notably the Gymnasium, the most likely route to higher education for academically inclined young Germans) were likely to be more proficient than their American counterparts in languages, history, and literature, as well as science. With such discrepancies in mind, he believed that the first two years of the American college must continue to build the groundwork of a liberal education by introducing students to tested truths about the physical and moral universe. In the second two years, there should still be strong guidance, if not total control, of the student's plan of study.

Eliot, on the other hand, regarded all this sort of thing as a drag on imagination and ambition. It raised the specter of a uniformly elementary curriculum "determined by the needs of the least capable students." It favored "superficiality" over "thoroughness," and violated the principle that "society is best served when every man's peculiar skill, faculty, or aptitude is developed and utilized to the highest possible degree."[33]

Neither man won the debate in the sense of carrying off a prize or compelling the loser's home institution to conform to the winner's view. But it is clear enough who got the best of it in the long run. At most colleges today, Eliot's approach is the norm. With the notable exception of St. John's College, very few limit their students' coursework to classic works of philosophy, literature, and science, while more than a few give students virtually unlimited freedom to study whatever they want. A couple of university-colleges, Columbia and Chicago, and a few independent colleges such as Ursinus College, try to split the difference along the lines of McCosh's model by requiring core courses of freshmen and sophomores in which, with the aid of classic texts, students (in the language of the current Ursinus catalogue), "reflect on the great questions of human existence . . . What does it mean to be human? How should we live our lives? What is the universe and how do we fit into it?"[34]

But most colleges today do neither. There might be some sort of freshman "gateway" course before students plunge into specialization or into a grab bag of unrelated subjects, and there is probably some loose "distribution" requirement that makes it hard, though probably not impossible, to study only one subject all the time. In other words, except for proselytizing institutions such as Bob Jones or Oral Roberts universities, very few colleges tell their students what to think. With equally rare exceptions, most are unwilling even to tell them what's worth thinking about.

4

Some tell the foregoing story as a tale of modernization achieved against the resistance of stubborn traditionalists like the actual Dr. McCosh or the fictional Professor Wagstaff ("Whatever it is, I'm against it"). Others tell it as a story of disintegration, to which resistance is noble but futile. Both versions have a share of truth and there is little to be gained by refighting the old battles—at least not outside particular institutions, since every college has its own culture and constituency and needs to come to its own accommodation between the needs and wants of its students, which are rarely the same thing.

Missing from both tellings is the fact that relatively little of this story has been driven by reflective consideration of what's best for college students. Despite a good deal of academic propaganda to the contrary, the fact is that when modern university leaders determine how to deploy resources, which "fields" to invest in, and so on, undergraduates tend to be of marginal consequence. As Clark Kerr put it, "undergraduate education in the large university is more likely to be acceptable than outstanding."[35] It is hard to imagine many presidents of major research universities today speaking about undergraduate education with Kerr's candor, not to mention the kind of concern and command of detail that McCosh and Eliot brought to their debate.

A relatively few college students (less than 1 percent of the total) still attend independent residential colleges that exist apart from a large university—but virtually all faculty, wherever or whomever they teach, have been trained in a university and so naturally bring their training with them into the undergraduate classroom. Seen in this wider view, McCosh doesn't quite deserve his reputation as crank and curmudgeon, and Eliot doesn't quite deserve his reputation as the Great Innovator. Long before he proclaimed the need for "Liberty in Education," the trend toward early specialization was already under way—driven not so much by high-minded concern for students as by the economic, demographic, and professional imperatives of the emerging university.

One force in favor of specialization (or, as some would prefer to call it, fragmentation) has always been the dependable fact that the size of the student body tends to increase. As Eliot acknowledged, a university "must have a large body of students, else many of its numerous courses of highly specialized instruction will find no hearers."[36] Growth is driven, too, by the unrelenting need for tuition revenue to support research activities, to generate funds for the provision of financial aid for needy students (to the extent that the institution is committed to what we nowadays call "socioeconomic diversity"), and to create an alumni base for future benefactions. For all these reasons, colleges, especially those within universities, almost always grow and seldom shrink, except for those that sometimes undershoot their enrollment targets. In the second half of the twentieth century, growth was also spurred by the spread of coeducation to previously all-male institutions that were loath to reduce their number of male students.[37] In the twenty-first century, it is being driven by the push to enroll more international students.

Sometimes the growth happens gradually, sometimes in spurts. In community colleges, for instance, enrollments have soared in the wake of the recent recession as young and not-so-young adults seek to retrain themselves for future employment. But at one pace or another, the upward trend in student numbers has been evident for at least 150 years—which, given the concurrent increase in the general population and the relatively smaller increase in the number of colleges, was and is inevitable. In 1869, aware of the growth imperative as he was taking office as Harvard's president, Eliot conceded that "one hundred and fifty young men cannot be so intimate with each other as fifty used to be." Growth, in other words, puts the collegiate ideal at risk. Yet by the time of his debate with McCosh in 1885, the number of freshmen at Harvard had doubled. In my own time at Columbia (I joined its faculty in 1985), the size of the college has grown by 50 percent. In seeking increased tuition revenue (urgent after the recession drove student financial need up and endowment income down) by admitting more students from the United States, as well as recruiting more from abroad, the college will no doubt continue to grow apace for the foreseeable future.

Why is growth generally bad for educational coherence? For one thing, in a curriculum that preserves even a few compulsory courses, the more students there are, the more the student population in these courses will exceed the supply of faculty able or willing to teach them. As one proponent of free course choice put it as long ago as 1825, "the old principle of requiring every student to pass through the hands of every instructor can no longer be wisely applied, since the time for the whole academic life has not been protracted."[38] This writer had in mind a bygone age when each compulsory subject—theology, classics, mathematics, history, and so on—had been taught by a single professor, under whom every student would therefore study at one time or another in his college career. Already by the 1840s, that kind of miniaturism had become a thing of the past at some institutions, and even the more modest goal of having every student follow a common course of study became elusive since, as the number of students grows, maintaining a compulsory curriculum means hiring an ever-larger number of faculty prepared to teach it.

Such a faculty is expensive to recruit and retain, especially in a competitive academic market, and in order for the curriculum to work well, those who teach it must work collaboratively in the sense of setting aside their particular research interests, doing "introductory" work with eighteen- and nineteen-year-olds, and talking with one another about what and how they are teaching. In effect, they have to unlearn what they learned—or at least make an effort to connect it with what others learned—in the university that trained them in their academic specialty.

Some institutions continue to foster this sort of collaborative teaching through introductory courses required of all undergraduates. To cite one impressive example, Ursinus College does so with its "Common Intellectual Experience" seminars, even though it has no graduate students to serve as teaching assistants. My own university—mainly because of pressure from adamant alumni, and with graduate students and postdocs increasingly carrying the load—still requires a demanding core curriculum of all college students, and at least some faculty who teach it discover that the gain in collegiality and self-education is worth the reduction of time for their scholarly pursuits. Keeping such courses—indeed, any courses—small comes at significant cost, so it is encouraging when a major institution moves away from the cost-efficient big-lecture model to smaller classes, as, for instance, the physics department at MIT has recently done, with the consequence of rising attendance and falling failure rates.[39]

Alternatively, an expanded college committed to some form of core education can herd students into large lectures delivered by willing faculty members on subjects that other faculty members have agreed should be taught—though not by themselves. Learning from a great lecturer can still be an exhilarating experience. This was the premise of the Harvard "Red Book" of 1945, which created a "General Education" program of basic courses in science, humanities, and social science taught by a few powerful lecturers who wanted to teach them. A vestige of that curriculum survives today in the form of such classes as Michael Sandel's famous course, "Justice," which regularly attracts something on the order of eight hundred students and serves them well. But Sandel, as the social scientists would say, is an outlier.

These problems of scale beset many colleges today. Behind them lies the more fundamental problem of the explosion of specialized knowledge. Already by the mid-nineteenth century, the hugely expanded scope of what was known about the world, particularly the natural world, had turned the once-respectable aspiration to master the main points of human knowledge (in the way, say, that Thomas Jefferson strove to educate himself over his lifetime) into an absurdity. As Eliot pointed out in his debate with McCosh, "out of the two hundred courses of instruction which stand on the list of Harvard University this year it would be difficult to select twenty which could have been given at the beginning of this century with the illustrations, materials, and methods now considered essential to the educational quality of the courses."[40] Two hundred was already a staggeringly higher number of courses than had been on offer just a few years earlier. Today, at every major university, there are thousands.

Both McCosh and Eliot recognized all the foregoing facts of modern academic life. McCosh wanted to resist them. Eliot wanted to embrace them. Both knew there was a price to pay for the twin expansions of student numbers and of the subjects and methods they could choose to study. Both expansions happened very rapidly. McCosh thought the price was too high and that paying it would make a coherent education impossible. Eliot thought it was the price of progress and had to be paid. They were both right.

5

Of the two forces—growth in student numbers and growth in knowledge—that have driven what the philosopher Alasdair MacIntyre calls the "divisive and fragmenting partitioning which contemporary academia imposes," the former may be slowed, but the latter is never likely to be arrested much less reversed. MacIntyre, who calls himself an "Augustinian Thomist," writes eloquently of the ideal university as "a community of enquiry" made up of a faculty with diverse interests but whose members agree on ultimate values.[41] But for today's faculty, apart from academic freedom—the freedom, that is, to pursue an inquiry of one's own choice and to have the result assessed by one's peers—it is hard to know what those values might be.

In fact, at any large university, the faculty is likely to cooperate across disciplinary lines—or even to show up in significant numbers for a general faculty meeting—only if academic freedom appears to be at risk or a budget crunch threatens the hiring of more faculty in one's home department. Serious collaboration in the work of educating undergraduates is rare. The recent failure at Harvard to enact meaningful reform of its college curriculum is the most visible case in point. After years of effort, the co-chair of the committee charged with shaping the reform commented drily: "We are just not accustomed to thinking about education in general terms. It's not our specialty."[42]

At Columbia, in the twenty years since the dissolution of the college faculty as a distinct entity within the larger faculty of arts and sciences—which now encompasses six schools, including graduate schools of the arts, and of international and public affairs—I am aware of only one faculty meeting where substantive discussion of undergraduate education took place. Led by a group of distinguished scientists who made a persuasive case for a new introductory science course to be added to the core curriculum, it was an exciting occasion. Unfortunately, however, a meeting such as the one I described in the preface to this book—where faculty discussed the financial aid program of the college in an informed and engaged way—would be extremely difficult to replicate today. And faculty disengagement (at Columbia, the faculty committee on college admissions and financial aid no longer exists) is by no means peculiar to certain institutions.[43] It is a natural, if not inevitable, consequence of the bureaucratization and what is sometimes called the "balkanization"—the splintering of the faculty into mutually wary interest groups—of modern academic life.

Against this fragmented reality, MacIntyre imagines an ideal university that looks a good deal like Newman's. Certain church-affiliated universities such as Notre Dame, where MacIntyre teaches, or, in their almost total commitment to scientific investigation, such institutions as the California Institute of Technology or Rockefeller University (which has no undergraduate students), do still aspire to such an ideal. But as a significant reality in the contemporary landscape of higher education, the university as community barely exists.

It hasn't for a long time. In an often-quoted comment, Robert Maynard Hutchins described the University of Chicago (of which he was president, then chancellor, from 1929 to 1951) as a miscellany of schools and departments "held together by a central heating system." A couple of decades later, Clark Kerr revised Hutchins's remark from a Californian's point of view when he described the Berkeley faculty as a "series of individual ... entrepreneurs held together by a common grievance over parking." The point is that the dominant force in the modern university has been centrifugal force—and it only became more so as the research university of the late nineteenth century gave way to what Kerr, in the mid-twentieth century, called the "multiversity."

As early as 1922, in his novel *Arrowsmith*, Sinclair Lewis described a vast institution whose name sounds like a blend of Wisconsin, Minnesota, and Michigan:

> The University of Winnemac ... has a baseball field
> under glass; its buildings are measured by the mile; it
> hires hundreds of young Doctors of Philosophy to give
> rapid instruction in Sanskrit, navigation, accountancy,
> spectacle-fitting, Sanitary engineering, Provençal poetry,
> tariff schedules, Rutabaga-growing, motor-car designing,
> the history of Voronezh, the style of Matthew Arnold,
> the diagnosis of *Myohypertrophia kymoparalytica*, and
> department-store advertising.

This is democratic education on a grand scale, the apotheosis of Ezra Cornell's dream of "an institution in which any person can find instruction in any study." It is also Kerr's multiversity before the fact—a prophetic instance of American gargantuanism, soon to be expressed in the supermarket and shopping mall, later in such unforeseeable inventions as Google and Wikipedia, which are capable of yielding infinite information but incapable of making distinctions of value.

When Lewis was writing nearly a century ago, his description of the university verged on parody, but today it seems perfectly plausible except that some of the "softer" subjects—"Provençal poetry," "the history of Voronezh"—have probably been cut from the curriculum. In our own time, the multiversity is fast becoming what the current president of Arizona State University, Michael Crow, calls the "Comprehensive Knowledge Enterprise" (CKE)—by which he means an international network of academic institutions, governments, aerospace, pharmaceutical, and biotech companies (among others) that collaborate on projects of common interest, often with the potential of large financial gain.

All these iterations of the modern university—from the German-style research institution of Eliot to the global abstraction of Michael Crow—have been driven overwhelmingly, if not exclusively, by science. As early as 1876, the inaugural president of Johns Hopkins, Daniel Coit Gilman (formerly a professor of geography), expressed what was happening when he defined not just the research mission but the teaching purpose of the new university as showing students "how to extend, even by minute accretions, the realm of knowledge." Eliot, a chemist, concurred: "One of the most important functions of universities," he wrote, is "to store up the accumulated knowledge of the race" so that "each successive generation of youth shall start with all the advantages which their predecessors have won." On this view, all of human history becomes a sort of relay race in which no runner is required to travel trodden ground.[44]

The efficacy of this principle is confirmed by the simple fact that, even before they get to college, well-prepared undergraduates today will have already mastered at least the first stages of calculus—this despite its having taken several millennia of recorded history before two seventeenth-century geniuses (Newton and Leibniz) invented the calculus in the first place. For the same reason, we expect a fourth-year medical student to know more, at, say, age twenty-six, about the genetic basis of disease or the management of organ transplantation than physicians knew twenty or even ten years ago. This progressive power of science is one of the astonishing achievements of human civilization. It does not mean that a bright young person with good schooling is more gifted than those of the past, but it is a stunning vindication of the premise that certain forms of knowledge are incremental and accretive—that once a new truth is discovered it does not have to be rediscovered but can be passed on to those capable of grasping and extending it.

For this reason, among others, science has an enormous advantage in the competition for university resources. It has the ability to demonstrate progress—an ability of inestimable value in a culture that has always been more forward-looking than retrospective. The idea of progress articulated in the late nineteenth century by Gilman and Eliot was the academic equivalent of what Frederick Winslow Taylor—whose influential book *Principles of Scientific Management* (1911) called for the rational distribution of specialized labor as essential for efficient industrial production—meant when he said that progress depends on making "real additions to the world's knowledge instead of reinventing things that are old."[45] This way of evaluating the worth of knowledge is consonant with how science works, and it poses a severe challenge to the humanities—at least to the extent that humanists remain concerned with preserving truth by rearticulating it rather than advancing truth by discarding the old in favor of the new.

Science also has the related advantage—though many good scientists object to this way of asserting the value of what they do—that it has led to innumerable technological advances visible to and appreciated by the public. Not only does it possess a means—the experimental method—by which its claims can be tested, but it has an obvious impact (not always benign, to be sure) on the lives of virtually everyone living and yet to be born. Transistors, computers, diagnostic machines, medical therapies, alternative sources of energy (we hope)—the list goes on and on of what constitutes, from one point of view, the "return" on public and private investment in higher education.

Such lists, although they may nod toward this or that historical or philosophical "breakthrough," are invariably dominated by scientific achievements, as in a recent book entitled *The Great American Research University*, whose list begins with the laser and magnetic resonance imaging and ends with Viagra.[46] If we include the social sciences under the same rubric, then science might also be credited with devising rational principles for legal and financial systems (though the latter has lately been called into question since very few academic economists foresaw the recent financial collapse), managing the infrastructure of transport and commerce, and promoting public health. In short, the university is the key institution that nurtures, exemplifies, and promotes a fundamental idea of modern culture: the idea of progress.

"Every century," Charles W. Eliot said with characteristic confidence, "has probably witnessed an unprecedented advance in civilization simply because the process is cumulative"—but before concluding his sentence he added a short qualifying clause, "if no catastrophes arrest it." It was an important addendum. Eliot had lived through the abolition of slavery, witnessed the advent of the telegraph, telephone, radio, and airplane, and arrived at the public celebration of his ninetieth birthday by automobile. He also lived long enough to witness the First World War in which, as Scott Fitzgerald (Princeton, class of 1917) put it, one empire walked forward "very slowly, dying in front and pushing forward behind" while "another empire walked very slowly backward a few inches a day, leaving the dead like a million bloody rugs." Within fifteen years of Eliot's death in 1926, a largely successful attempt was under way to exterminate the Jews of Europe using modern organizational techniques and carried out by the nation whose universities were arguably the world's best.

6

How has the modern university taken account of such realities?

Science is no help here. Its principle of progress does not, as the phrase goes, "translate well" into the study of culture and historical experience. Yet, as Julie Reuben recounts in a valuable book, *The Making of the Modern University: Intellectual Transformation and the Marginalization of Morality*, it became "the primary aim" throughout the university "to train students to think "scientifically."[47] The power of the scientific paradigm has been so great that humanistic or liberal studies, which have always properly included science, have tried to adapt it for their own purposes.

This is what MacIntyre calls "a mimicking of the technical in areas where it has in fact no application."[48] Early in the history of the modern university, humanists mimicked scientists by trying to describe language as if it could be studied in much the way their scientific colleagues studied the properties of gas or light in the lab next door. The discipline of philology yielded some good results for understanding the structure of language and affinities among languages. Carefully researched biographical studies proved useful for illuminating the lives of historical figures, and the sum of human knowledge was increased by the painstaking transcription of unpublished documents and the establishment of reliable texts by collation with variant versions. This was the era, too, of "scientific" history—the idea that empirical investigation could establish laws that govern human behavior over time with no less consistency and predictability than, say, the laws of physics.

But scientists rarely took these flattering imitations very seriously, and humanists had their private doubts. The literary scholar Alvin Kernan tells a delicious story about his experience at Oxford, where he studied English soon after the Second World War. Kernan's tutor, watching his nervous American tutee struggle with the technicalities of "linguistic science," took pity on him and offered this advice: "When you hit a word in a text that you cannot identify, simply correlate it with some modern word that it sounds like and then invent a bridge between them. Most of the examiners will be suspicious, but may consider, so imprecise is linguistic science, your little word history an interesting possibility." As for "scientific" history, it led to more confusion than resolution, as when a respected historian of World War I, writing in the 1920s, expressed dismay at how he and a fellow scholar could have arrived at opposite conclusions from the same evidence: "This has always troubled me. We had both taken advanced degrees at eminent universities. . . . We used the same documents and read the same biographies and memoirs in preparing our respective books—and came up with quite different interpretations. . . . Is there something wrong with our methods?"[49]

By the later twentieth century, those days of chasing the phantom of objectivity had been left behind. If humanists had once tried emulating the scientists, now they repudiated them. They denied the very idea of truth by asserting, with varying degrees of "postmodern" irony, that all putative truths are contingent and all values relative. Yet the result was the same: the humanities continued to marginalize themselves in the universities and therefore, by the "trickle-down" effect, in the colleges.

Today, the pendulum seems to be swinging back toward scientism—a vivid instance of what MacIntyre calls the "change of fashion rather than progress" that characterizes the academic humanities. At Stanford's Center for the Study of the Novel, for example, there is now a "literature lab" where teams of graduate students perform searches of digitized texts looking for patterns of recurrent words that signal shifts in theme or style over the long history of prose fiction. The procedure is known as "distant reading"—reading, that is, by machines that can scan much larger databases (numbers of novels) than any human reader could possibly handle. The ultimate goal is for scholars to "stop reading books and start counting, graphing and mapping them instead."[50] This kind of work may, in time, yield useful results for cultural historians, but one can only imagine where it will leave undergraduates who have even an incipient interest in reading the old way.

For most college students, the point of college has never had much to do with what goes on in the university world of research or professional controversy—pro-science or anti-science or otherwise. Nor does the principle of scientific progress have much to offer the humanities—except, perhaps, as an episode in the history of ideas and a challenge for thinking about questions of value. We cannot say that Defoe's *Journal of a Plague Year*, published in 1722, or Camus's *La Peste*, in 1947, tells us more about the social consequences of pestilence than did Thucydides in his fifth-century BCE commentary on the plague at Athens. Or that Joyce's *Ulysses*, written at the outset of the twentieth century, gives a more complete account of experience than did *The Odyssey*, probably composed more than two and a half millennia earlier.

Science, moreover, tells us nothing about how to shape a life or how to face death, about the meaning of love, or the scope of responsibility. It not only fails to answer such questions; it cannot ask them. Some people believe that someday it will do both—that in some future age of "consilience," neuroscience will define and ensure happiness and prove or disprove the insights of religion into the nature of sin and salvation; biochemistry will distinguish truth from falsity among what today are mere opinions about sex and gender; indeed all human choices will become susceptible to experimental testing and rational sorting. Maybe it will happen, but none of us will be around when it does, and it's not clear that we would want to be.

Meanwhile, literature, history, philosophy, and the arts are becoming the stepchildren of our colleges.[51] This is a great loss because they are the legatees of religion in the sense that they provide a vocabulary for formulating ultimate questions of the sort that have always had special urgency for young people. In fact, the humanities may have the most to offer to students who do not know that they need them—which is one reason it is scandalous to withhold them. One of the ironies of contemporary academic life is that even as the humanities become marginal in our colleges, they are establishing themselves in medical, law, and business schools, where interest is growing in the study of literature and the arts as a way to encourage self-critical reflection among future physicians, attorneys, and entrepreneurs. It is ironic, too, that amid rising concern over America's competitive position in the global "knowledge economy," we hear more and more about the need for technical training, and less and less about the value of liberal education at home, even as the latter gains adherents among our competitors abroad.[52]

It will always be hard to state the value of such an education in a succinct or summary way. Yet many people, if given half a chance, discover it for themselves. For one thing, great works of art can be antidotes to loneliness. A moving expression of this truth is a recent book by the poet Rachel Hadas, about her husband's descent into dementia, in which she recalls how literature provided her with companions more attuned to her torment than even her closest friends—as when she read a poem by Philip Larkin that captured her experience lying beside the diminished man with whom she had once laughed and loved:

> Talking in bed ought to be easiest,
> Lying together there goes back so far,
> An emblem of two people being honest.
>
> Yet more and more time passes silently.
> Outside, the wind's incomplete unrest
> Builds and disperses clouds about the sky.
>
> And dark towns heap up on the horizon.
> None of this cares for us. Nothing shows why
> At this unique distance from isolation
>
> It becomes still more difficult to find
> Words at once true and kind
> Or not untrue and not unkind.[53]

Literature has the power, too, to contract space and time. When I first read *The Iliad* with a group of Columbia freshmen, there came a moment after all our discussion of Homeric similes and the formulaic structure of oral poetry and the mythic origin of national identity, when we suddenly felt as if we were reading about ourselves—or at least, if we were male—our childhood selves. It happened when we arrived at the image with which Homer describes (in Richmond Lattimore's translation) how Trojan soldiers overran their Greek enemies: "They streamed over / in massed formation with Apollo in front of them holding / the tremendous aegis, and wrecked the bastions of the Achaians easily, as when a little boy piles sand by the sea-shore / when in his innocent play he makes sand towers to amuse him / and then, still playing, with hands and feet ruins them and wrecks them." Apparently, little boys on the shores of the Aegean three thousand years ago did the same thing that little boys do today at Jones Beach or the Hamptons.

Whatever the explanation for such transhistorical truths, certain books—old and not so old—speak to us in a subversive whisper that makes us wonder whether the idea of progress might be a sham. They tell us that the questions we face under the shadow of death are not new, and that no new technology will help us answer them. As much as the questions posed by science, these are hard and serious questions, and should be part of every college education. Does Achilles' concept of honor in *The Iliad* retain any force for us today? What would it mean truly to live according to Thoreau's ethic of minimal exploitation of nature, or by Kant's categorical imperative? Is there a basis in experience for the Augustinian idea of original sin? Such questions do not admit of verifiable or replicable answers because the experiment to which we must subject them is the experiment of our own lives.

FOUR

WHO WENT? WHO GOES?

WHO PAYS?

The modern university was an entirely new entity—in part an educational institution focused on graduate and professional training, but in larger part a research enterprise driven by science. Where, in this house of many mansions, was the college? Did it—does it—still exist as a place of guided self-discovery for young people in search of themselves?

One way of coming at this question was suggested around a century ago by Max Weber, who, not long before Sinclair Lewis invented "Winnemac," proposed a distinction between two "polar opposites of types of education." The types he had in mind correspond closely to the terms "college" and "university" as I have been using them. The first, associated with religion, is "to aid the novice to acquire a 'new soul' ... and hence, to be reborn." The second, associated with the bureaucratic structures of modern life, is to impart the kind of "specialized expert training" required for "administrative purposes—in the organization of public authorities, business offices, workshops, scientific or industrial laboratories," as well as "disciplined armies."[1] Many other service-able terms could be substituted for Weber's—knowledge versus skill; inspiration versus discipline; insight versus information; learning for its own sake versus learning for the sake of utility—but whatever terms we prefer, a good educational institution strives for both. "The two types do not stand opposed," as Weber put it, "with no connections or transitions between them." They coexist—or at least they should—in a dynamic relation.

Beginning with the rise of the research university and continuing ever since, American higher education has struggled to maintain this dialectic. For good or ill, the oldest and richest institutions have been looked to as models, so it mattered for more than Harvard when the president who succeeded Eliot, Abbott Lawrence Lowell, decided that the college was being overwhelmed by the centrifugal force of the university, and that something had to be done about it.

In the early 1920s, with the help of a $13 million gift (at least $150 million in today's dollars) from the Harkness family, Lowell oversaw the creation of undergraduate "houses," each with resident faculty, dining hall, common rooms, and library. Yale initially declined a gift from the same source for the same purpose, but soon reversed itself and built a comparable cluster of what, with more explicit deference to the Oxbridge originals, it called "colleges." More than a decade earlier, at Princeton, Woodrow Wilson, president from 1901 to 1910, had attempted something similar, but he failed in part because Princeton students had long organized themselves into "eating clubs" that provided, according to tradition-minded alumni, sufficient social coherence. In fact, by sorting students according to class and caste, the clubs reflected what one enterprising reporter for the *Harvard Crimson*, after a field trip to Princeton, called its "frank institutionalization of arbitrary and unreflective prejudices."[2]

Wilson failed to dislodge these prejudices, some of which he doubtless shared; but he did succeed in hiring, at great expense, scores of new tutors or "preceptors" with the aim of bringing students into a "mind and mind" relation with their teachers as well as with each other rather than leaving them to sit in silent rows in lecture halls.[3] To this day, the size of "precepts" at Princeton—the discussion sections attached to lecture courses—is capped at fourteen. At relatively less wealthy institutions (compared with Harvard, Yale, and Princeton), such as Chicago and Columbia, resistance to the fragmenting pull of the university took the form of core curricula in which undergraduates were expected to anchor their education.

A main goal of all these reforms was to preserve what I have called lateral learning. Long before the creation of the Yale residential colleges, that quintessential—if fictional—Yalie, Dink Stover, remarked that the point of college was "to educate ourselves by knowing opposite lives."[4] Looking back at Stover's era, we tend to dismiss his conception of "opposite" as absurdly narrow—a version of what Freud famously called "the narcissism of minor differences." We imagine young men in V-necks and plaid slacks who speak with the crooning intonation of Rudy Vallee (Yale '27) and who all hail from the same social set, where "opposite" means the difference between growing up in an uptown brownstone as opposed to a downtown duplex, or summering in Newport instead of on the Cape.

The inbreeding was never actually as extreme as the caricature suggests (Vallee was the child of immigrants—a French Canadian father and an Irish mother), but, in effect, by the early twentieth century the Big Three, or, as they are known today, "HYP," had made a pact with the country club crowd: in return for your loyalty, attested by your gifts and bequests, we will admit your sons, and we'll do so, at least conditionally, even if the boy isn't quite up to snuff. Mark Twain, who had a keen eye for the tribal practices of the eastern elite, tells us in *Pudd'nhead Wilson* that the pampered Missouri boy who goes up to Yale arrives there "handsomely equipped with 'conditions'." He has been accepted, that is, on condition that he will eventually pass examinations in subjects he has failed to master at school.[5]

This sort of provisional pass was part of "a policy of vigorous affirmative action for the privileged," as one historian has called it, though not everyone within the circle of privilege supported the policy unreservedly.[6] Charles W. Eliot was known to rail against making allowances for "the stupid sons of the rich," and under his leadership, slowly but surely, the intellectual standards of the university undermined—or overcame, depending on one's point of view—the social values of the college.[7] At least in Twain's fictional world, trading family status for a Yale degree was not quite a done deal: the dull boy flunks out and is sent home with "manners much improved" but "as indolent as ever."

The process of raising standards, as we would call it today, meant taking in talent regardless of social origin. But opening up college to previously excluded groups has always been a process of ebb and flow, and academic leaders have been divided within, as well as among, themselves about how far or fast to go. When it came to admitting undergraduates, Nicholas Murray Butler, president of Columbia for virtually the whole first half of the twentieth century, favored a Jewish quota; but he also pressured the old boys of the English Department to grant tenure to a brilliant young Columbia College graduate, Lionel Trilling, whom they had written off as a Marxist, a Freudian, and, most damningly, a Jew.[8]

At Harvard, mindful of the "Jewish invasion" that ruined Columbia in the eyes of its blue-blood alumni, Lowell, too, clamped down on admitting Jewish students, suspecting they were long on brains but short on "character." He also favored excluding Harvard's few black students from its freshmen residence halls, and, in his role as public figure, supported restrictive immigration laws. Yet Lowell's motive in creating the house system was to close the divide between wealthy and needy students. He was appalled to see rich boys segregating themselves in "gold coast" apartments while those with less money were relegated to rooming houses where they paid the rent by working a (usually) menial campus job. "Snobbish separation . . . on lines of wealth," he felt, threatened "to destroy the chief value of the College as a place for the training of character."[9]

Lowell's innovation hardly put an end, of course, to cliquishness or class stratification. One lightly fictionalized memoir from the 1930s reports "how similar the faces always looked in the Varsity picture, except where there was an Irishman or a Jew, and even then they seemed somehow anglicized down toward alikeness." And lest some "anglicized" Irishman or Jew contaminate the race by means of an unwary Beacon Hill belle, one enterprising college bureaucrat ran a brisk business selling "the addresses of selected Anglo-Saxon sophomores to the mothers of Boston debutantes."[10] Until the outbreak of the Second World War, such fictions had the plausibility of fact. Through midcentury, accommodations in the Harvard houses were of variable price, depending on size and location, and the few commuting students (often Jews from Roxbury or Dorchester) were known as "meatballs."[11] As late as the 1970s, one of the jobs performed by Harvard students in return for financial aid was cleaning the bathrooms of classmates, for which, when such a student arrived with mop and pail, he could expect to be rewarded by being called behind his back—or even to his face—"toilet man."

In short, over roughly the first two-thirds of the twentieth century, there persisted at elite colleges a strong current of social snobbery as well as an undercurrent of anti-intellectualism—not to mention outright racism and anti-Semitism. But the flow was tidal. It did not go always and only in one direction, and when the tide was coming in at one institution, it might be going out at another. By 1953, upon the retirement of Lowell's successor, James Bryant Conant, nearly a third of Harvard freshmen were on scholarship—around twice the fraction that typically would have received financial aid a hundred years earlier. By 1957, under the new president, Nathan Marsh Pusey, the fraction had declined to barely a fifth. In the midst of the Second World War, nearly two-thirds of Princeton undergraduates opposed the admission of black students. (The first black student to earn a Princeton BA was in the class of 1947.) By the end of the war, at Yale, roughly 90 percent favored a drive to raise scholarship funds on behalf of black students. At Columbia, as late as the late 1960s, security guards routinely checked the IDs of black students while allowing whites—students or not—to come and go around campus as they pleased.[12]

2

We tend to look back at this exclusionary history with a combination of incredulity and indignation, and to praise the present at the expense of the past. There are good grounds to do so. Admissions procedures originally devised as ways to screen out Jews—personal essays, letters of recommendation, interviews—are touted today as ways to identify qualities that may not be captured by grades or tests. Formerly excluded groups such as blacks or Hispanics, once virtually barred from many institutions, are now beneficiaries of "race-conscious" admissions policies. College, we say, used to be about preserving uniformity, but today it is about achieving diversity.

How we got from one to the other is a stirring story. It has many chapters, of which the democratizing of elite institutions is only one—and, as a matter of scale, a minor one. At the turn of the century, when Stover was prepping for Yale, fewer than a quarter-million Americans, or around 2 percent of the population between eighteen and twenty-four, attended college. By the end of World War II, that figure had risen to over two million. In 1975, it stood at nearly ten million, or one-third of young adults. Today, including those students whom we call "nontraditional," the number has almost doubled.

This enormous advance in college attendance was the sum of many incremental advances: the founding of women's colleges and "Negro" colleges in the late nineteenth century; the expansion of land-grant colleges into a constellation of state universities on the scale of "Winnemac"; the adoption in the 1950s of Clark Kerr's California "master plan," with its three-tiered system of community colleges, state colleges, and research universities aimed at providing virtually universal higher education for an exploding population; the breakdown of racial barriers, first by voluntary, then compulsory, integration, and later by what has come to be known as affirmative action; and the rise of coeducation in formerly all-male private institutions. All these advances promoted the development of what is now conventionally called "human capital" and, according to many economists, deserve a good deal of credit for America's rise in the twentieth century to world dominance.[13] Some people believe that the next chapter is being written by purveyors of "distance learning" via the Internet and, despite abuses that have lately come to light, by entrepreneurs of education for profit.

In fact, the story is older than any of these elements. It goes back to church-sponsored scholarships for promising schoolboys in the seventeenth and eighteenth centuries. Recognizing God's freedom to favor the poor and damn the rich, seventeenth-century Puritans assumed no reliable alignment between the condition of a person's soul and the worldly rank into which he or she was born. In the eighteenth century, writers of democratic sentiment held that "maids, shoemakers, and cooks" had "more native intelligence than the upper classes allowed them to express."[14] In other words, it has long been recognized that human capital is widely distributed among social classes and does not correlate with conditions of birth or with social status. "Many a Rittenhouse," one Yale graduate declared in 1781, is to be found "among our Mechanick genii," and "an American Cincinnatus upon every farm."[15] A hundred years later, Harvard's president vowed that "no good student need ever stay away from Cambridge or leave college simply because he is poor," while the president of the University of North Dakota (founded in 1883) provided interest-free loans to needy students from his personal bank account.[16]

But it has always been easier to proclaim these principles than to put them into practice. Still, by the second third of the twentieth century it was no longer possible to speak of "the college bred" as if they were race horses or show dogs—certainly not after 1944, when Congress passed the GI Bill (officially, the Servicemen's Readjustment Act) with the intent of avoiding a repetition of the social unrest that followed World War I, when veterans returned to a labor market that could not absorb them. The GI Bill brought onto campuses throughout the nation—including the most elite—students whose fathers would have once set foot there only as janitors or kitchen help. It made "reasonable the pursuit of careers that, before the war, were unrealistic even if perceived, and that older siblings simply never aspired to."[17] It made a huge difference in the tone of college life (nearly three-quarters of students entering Harvard in 1946 had served in the military), and, in the larger population, helped to turn what had been a class divide into a generational divide.[18] As one character—an almost elderly businessman—says with mild resentment in Arthur Miller's play *All My Sons* (1947), nowadays you can "stand on a streetcorner and spit, and you're liable to hit a college man."

The most important force in democratizing American higher education was the explosive postwar growth of what had once been known as junior colleges—two-year institutions whose origins were in the "normal schools" that had been founded in the nineteenth century and flourished early in the twentieth, and whose primary focus had been on training schoolteachers. For some students, these institutions served as conduits to a nearby or affiliated university where graduates of a two-year college could go on to earn the bachelor's degree. By the 1950s, the junior colleges were evolving into a national system of what are now known as community colleges, which today number more than twelve hundred, with an enrollment exceeding six million— roughly a third of all undergraduates in the United States. In California, under Kerr's master plan, community colleges were designed as entry points into a system of higher education that provided students with the opportunity, if they did well in their first two years, to advance to one of the four-year state colleges or even to a research university.

Meanwhile, private and selective public institutions made increasing use of standardized tests for the purpose of identifying talented students outside their usual "feeder" schools. Also in the

1950s, the Ivies established the principle of "need-based" financial aid.[19] This was an effort to replace the scattershot philanthropy of the past, by which scholarships had been awarded on somebody's hunch about who deserved what, with a rational system of discount pricing based on careful evaluation of what a family could afford. It was a push for distributive justice—or, some might say, a dose of socialism ("each according to his need")—in a world otherwise run according to the rules of the market.

At the wealthiest institutions, need-based aid was followed by a policy that came to be known as "need-blind admissions"—a combination still limited today to some fifty colleges with substantial endowments. In theory, at least, this means that a "firewall" goes up between the admissions office and the financial aid office. In the former, candidates are assessed without regard to economic means. In the latter, once the admissions office has decided which students to admit, the amount is calculated that each successful candidate can afford to pay based on financial disclosure by the family, and an aid "package" (grants, loans, campus job) is offered to make up the difference between the cost of attendance and what the family can contribute—though not every college with "need-blind" or "need-based" policies is equally scrupulous in meeting the full need of all the students it admits. Especially if a college makes a serious effort to recruit students of modest means, these two policies in tandem can be extremely expensive to implement. It's no accident that they emerged in the postwar years when the economy was booming, demands for social justice rising, and the struggle against socialism in its Soviet form seemed to require that colleges nurture talent wherever they could find it.

Progress in the public universities was even more remarkable, both in expanding opportunity for low-income and first-generation college students, and in supporting first-class teaching and research across all fields. Over the first half of the twentieth century, Brooklyn College and the City College of New York established themselves among the most intellectually vibrant institutions in the world. At midcentury, the University of California at Berkeley challenged and in some respects exceeded HYP in both accessibility and quality, while the flagship branches of other state universities such as Ohio, Michigan, Wisconsin, Indiana, Illinois, and, more recently, Texas, North Carolina, Oregon, Washington, and Florida, rose into the ranks of the world's leading institutions. And in many cases, these huge institutions have sought to provide a true residential experience for undergraduate students. The America that Alexis de Tocqueville had described in the early nineteenth century as a nation where "primary education is within the reach of everyone" but "higher education is within the reach of virtually no one" seemed to be turning itself upside down.[20]

3

The foregoing story is usually told as a triumphant one. But there are a number of things wrong with it. For one thing, it fits too neatly the progressive narrative we like to tell about ourselves. Need-blind admissions, for instance, is an admirable ideal, but it can be little more than a feel-good slogan if a college concentrates its recruiting in places like Scarsdale or Riyadh, where it won't encounter candidates with much need. As one college president told me when I first tried to understand these policies, "If you really want to practice need-blind admissions, cover up the zip codes when the applications come in." Campus interviews may seem to be about, as the phrase goes, getting to know the whole person, but since they are often conducted by alumni volunteers or student interns with little input into the ultimate decision, they tend to be, as the Stanford sociologist Mitchell Stevens calls them in a book entitled *Creating a Class*, "heavily symbolic"— designed "as much to affirm the college's commitment to personalized evaluation as to learn more about applicants."[21]

Nor is it clear that racial or ethnic discrimination is entirely behind us. In *The Price of Admission: How America's Ruling Class Buys Its Way into Elite Colleges—and Who Gets Left Outside the Gates*, Daniel Golden has argued that today's "new Jews" are Asian Americans, whom, judging by grades and tests alone, one should expect to find in greater numbers at some of the most selective private colleges. Even allowing for regional differences and group inclination toward this or that institution, there is a striking discrepancy between, say, the percentage of Asian American students at Berkeley (almost 50 percent), where scores and grades count overwhelmingly, and Princeton (under 20 percent) where "personal qualities" figure in the mix.[22] Something would seem to be wrong with this picture—although at both Berkeley, which draws its undergraduates mainly from California (whose residents are roughly 13 percent of Asian background) and Princeton, which draws more broadly on the whole nation (in which the corresponding figure is around 5 percent), Asian Americans are being admitted at a rate roughly three times their proportion to the relevant base population. If conscious discrimination does still exist, the historical experience of Jews, Catholics, and other once-dreaded minorities suggests that it will abate over time.

Less likely to be resolved anytime soon are the pervasive problems that low-income students face not only in gaining admission to elite colleges but in getting to and through college at all. One leading authority, Donald Heller of Pennsylvania State University, asserts that "college-going rates of the highest-socioeconomic-status students with the lowest achievement levels are the same as the poorest students with the highest achievement levels."[23] This sobering statement doesn't tell us much about the advantages or obstacles (adequate or inadequate financial resources; stable or broken families; strong or weak schools) that help or hurt a student's chances of getting to college; and it is striking that children growing up in economically deprived circumstances who attend good high schools do much better than those in poor schools—although they still lag significantly behind their wealthier peers.[24] But however one slices the data, it is clear that the progressive story of expanding opportunity has slowed or stalled, and there is reason to doubt that the United States can truly be described today as a nation of equal opportunity where talent and effort trump poverty and prejudice.

One reason for the slowdown can be traced to the late 1970s, when California's Proposition 13 (1978) initiated a series of populist tax revolts that became chronic tax resistance, and eventually led, state by state, to "massive disinvestment" in higher education.[25] The University of Virginia, for example, founded by Thomas Jefferson for the public welfare, has recently been described as "a public university in name only" since it now receives a mere 8 percent of its funding from the state of Virginia, down from nearly 30 percent a quarter century ago.[26] At the University of Wisconsin, in a state with a long progressive tradition, only about 19 percent comes from public funds—also down from around 30 percent just a decade ago. To make up for the decline in public money, tuition rates at public universities have been climbing even faster than at private institutions—a trend likely to accelerate, while state universities are also recruiting increasing numbers of out-of-state students, who pay higher tuition than in-state residents. To make matters worse over the past couple of decades, financial aid to individual students administered by the states has been allocated more and more on the basis of so-called merit rather than need. (Between 1999 and 2009, merit aid grew by more than 150 percent, while need-based aid rose by less than 100 percent.)[27] This means that scholarships have been going increasingly to high-achieving students who come disproportionately from high-income families, leaving deserving students from low-income families without the means to pay for college.

The same shift of support from more needy to less needy students has been evident at the federal level. In 1976, the maximum federal Pell grant for a low-income student covered nearly 90 percent of the average cost of attending a four-year public institution, and almost 40 percent at a private university. By 2004, Pell grants covered under 25 percent of the cost at a public college, and less than 10 percent at a private institution. And while funding of grants for low-income students has failed to keep up with the rising cost of college, there has been robust growth in the amount of unsubsidized federal loans that go mainly to students from middle-income families.[28] Before the election of 2010, President Obama and the Democratic Congress were trying to reverse this trend by enhancing Pell grants and turning them into an entitlement whose value would keep pace with inflation. But with tax revenues falling and tuitions continuing to rise, and now with the government in a deficit-cutting mood, such initiatives seem likely to be rolled back—although at this writing (August 2011), the Pell grant program has been spared in the first deficit-reduction deal.

As for private institutions, at least since the rise of need-based aid in the middle years of the last century, the prevailing financial model has been a "Robin Hood" system whereby relatively affluent students pay a larger share of college costs than needier students—something some parents find objectionable. "Why should I pay full freight when Johnny's roommate is getting a free ride?" is a question familiar to financial aid officers. It is usually asked in ignorance of the fact that even families paying full "sticker price" (now over $50,000 at the most expensive colleges) are meeting far less than the full cost of their child's education—calculated as a proportional fraction of faculty and staff salaries, dining, library, health, and athletic services, as well as overhead costs such as keeping the lights on, the heat flowing, and the buildings in good repair. In other words, all students, rich and poor, in America's private colleges—except at those run for profit—are subsidized to one extent or another.[29] What this means for the college is that it must make up the difference between operating costs and tuition revenue with other sources of income such as endowment return, government grants, and private donations.

Since the crash of 2008, this has become much harder to do. Endowments, government support, and the amount of giving have all fallen or are rising more slowly, while pressure on financial aid budgets has sharply increased. This is not a pretty symmetry, and it puts financial aid offices under heavy strain to keep up with demand.[30] Even those parents who have not lost their jobs have probably seen their retirement assets dwindle and the value of their homes drop, leaving them ineligible for home equity or other loans that were once among their options for financing their children's education.

At the same time, the colleges themselves also feel squeezed—and not just financially. They are under constant scrutiny by trustees, alumni, and the general public, all of whom keep a keen eye on the college rankings, of which those published in *U.S. News & World Report* are the most closely watched. Those who compile these rankings claim to base them on salient measures such as graduation and retention rates, "selectivity" (the percentage of applicants to whom offers of admission are made), faculty compensation, alumni giving, peer assessment, among others—but what they really express is the cumulative impression summed up by the word "prestige." Thorstein Veblen noted long ago that American higher education has much in common with "a circus, theatrical or operatic enterprise" whose ticket sales depend on the fame of the acrobats or the leading man or leading lady—of which the academic equivalents are the faculty, student athletes, and president.[31]

So the quest for prestige is nothing new, but it has lately reached such frantic intensity that it is having seriously negative effects on the educational mission of many institutions. For one thing, it means that at some colleges, the quality of the educational experience is confused with how many applicants it turns away. And since a lower acceptance rate means higher prestige, the quest for more and more applicants becomes relentless—not primarily for the purpose of finding "better" students (at the most selective schools, a great many valedictorians with perfect GPAs and SATs are already turned down) but in order to ballyhoo how hard it is to get in. Colleges are less eager, however, to put out the news that some applicants will find it harder than others. Recruited athletes, alumni children, faculty children, members of historically underrepresented minority groups, and "development cases" (children of generous donors) have an advantage, and by the time they have all been accounted for, the number of slots remaining can be extremely small compared with the ever-growing applicant pool. In short, the admissions culture of selective colleges today is characterized by a rising degree of deception and—no doubt, unintended—cruelty.[32]

Another problem—or, rather, part of the problem—is the obsessive concern with test scores, which have limited predictive value for what individual students will learn in, or contribute to, college, but a lot to do with reducing access for students from low-income families. Moreover, as the psychologist Robert J. Sternberg has written, tests and grades signify little about "a student's overall potential to make a positive difference in the world." It is also well known that SAT scores correlate closely with socioeconomic family standing. The total average SAT score of students from families earning more than $100,000 per year is over a hundred points higher than for students in the income range of $50,000 to $60,000.[33] Theoretically, such a correlation could mean that intelligence (whatever that is) closely tracks how much money one's parents make. But that inference should seem doubtful even to the most confirmed Social Darwinist. More likely, it means that parents with money have ways to inflate their children's scores—by living in an affluent neighborhood, for example, with good public or private schools.

Such parents also have the option of providing SAT prep help for their children and buying the services of private college advisors, while low-income students not only lack access to such advantages, but typically attend high schools that offer little or no college counseling. For them, the fees incurred by submitting multiple applications or even the cost of visiting a college away from home can be prohibitive. And yet, without compunction, one Ivy League alumni magazine recently carried an ad for an "intensive 4-day . . . college application boot camp" run by a former admissions officer, at a price of $14,000. Another service called "IvyWise," known for its "platinum package" of tutoring and counseling, charged $30,000—and that was a few years ago.[34]

4

Ticking off such inequities is easy to do, and creates opportunities for righteously condemning individual and institutional behavior. Yet all these practices raise difficult ethical questions—of just the sort, in fact, that should be part of a college education.[35] How many of us with the means to help would look our own son or daughter in the eye and say, "I will put you at a disadvantage by refusing to spend our family's money helping you prep for the test"? And while it's natural to feel resentment when other people's children enjoy advantages denied to our own, for centuries very few people objected to what amounted to affirmative action for whites. Most of the beneficiaries took their preferential standing for granted, while most of the excluded were remarkably gracious about their exclusion. Today, however, a lot of people object to affirmative action for minorities, which as Anthony Kronman puts it, entails "a contest of right against right—a conflict between the defensible claim of minority applicants to a form of special treatment and the equally defensible claim of non-minority applicants to be judged by their individual qualifications alone." Nor is affirmative action for alumni children (though it is rarely called by that name) a simple matter of right or wrong. Not many colleges can afford to alienate loyal alumni, on whose benefactions they depend for educating all students—including low-income students—by turning away their (qualified) children in larger numbers than they already do.[36]

The more one delves into the intricacies of selective college admissions, the more such questions force themselves into view. Is it legitimate to offer lower aid to students who seem likely to accept an offer of admission (alumni children, for example, or candidates who have proven their zeal by traveling a long way to campus for an interview), and thereby conserve the budget for students who might need to be "incentivized" to enroll? Should a wealthy institution offer grants instead of loans to all students whom it deems eligible for any amount of financial aid, so they won't be deterred by debt from pursuing relatively low-paying careers in, say, teaching or public service? Or, given the market value of its prestigious degree, should such an institution reserve grants for the more needy students and stick with loans for the less needy, who probably won't have much trouble paying back whatever they have borrowed? Is it a fair use of resources to provide extraordinary aid to families making as much as $200,000 per year (as Harvard and Yale announced they would do before the crash of 2008) in view of the ensuing pressure on less wealthy colleges to follow suit, thereby leaving themselves unable to offer adequate support to needier students? One former Harvard dean, Theda Skocpol, put this dilemma in the form of a stinging question: Why should America's leading universities make "the annual cost for families up to the 95th income percentile less than half the cost of purchasing a new luxury car"?[37]

And what about programs that offer, in exchange for submitting an early application and a promise to attend if admitted, a better chance of getting in? One argument in favor of such programs, which are increasingly popular, is that they bring to campus every fall a freshman class made up in large part of students happy to be at their first-choice college. Another favorable argument, though rarely acknowledged in public, is that locking in half the class early (decisions are announced before Christmas) allows the college to be more selective in choosing among candidates who apply later, and thereby improve its ranking in *U.S. News & World Report*. A counterargument—which Harvard and Princeton at first dismissed, then endorsed when they briefly ended their early admissions programs, and now, having resumed them, reject once again—is that such programs "advantage the already advantaged" who are well-prepped for the admissions process and whose financial resources allow them to zero in on a single college without waiting to see if its financial aid offer will make it possible to attend.[38]

None of these questions—and there are many more—has an ethically simple answer. What's beyond dispute is that the practices they bring into view are heavily weighted in favor of students from families with means. Before the economic debacle of 2008, a national discussion seemed to be getting under way about ways to respond to this inequity, which was clearly growing. Between the mid-1970s and mid-1990s, in a sample of eleven prestigious colleges, the percentage of students from families in the bottom quartile of national family income remained roughly steady—around 10 percent. During the same period the percentage of students from the top quartile rose sharply, from a little more than one-third to fully half. And if the sample is broadened to include the top 150 colleges as designated by the *Chronicle of Higher Education*, the percentage of students from the bottom quartile drops to around 3 percent.[39]

There are many reasons for dismay at this situation, one of which was stated by former Princeton president William Bowen, who wrote in 2005 that "the sense of democratic legitimacy is undermined if people believe that the rich are admitted to selective colleges and universities regardless of merit while able and deserving candidates from more modest backgrounds are turned away."[40] As a step toward restoring some sense of legitimacy, Bowen proposed that academically promising students from low-income families get "a thumb on the scale"—an advantage comparable to what alumni children, athletes, and minority candidates already get. If they have lower test scores or fewer AP classes of the sort that high schools in the inner city or in rural areas rarely offer, these deficiencies should be considered in the context of limited opportunities, and evidence of success in overcoming obstacles should also be taken into account. Proposals of this sort were responses to the fact that at most private selective colleges, the already-small enrollment of low-income students was getting smaller even before the financial crash, when endowments were soaring. But they have been put into practice at only a very few elite institutions, notably Harvard and also Amherst, which, during the presidency of Anthony Marx (2003–2011), recruited aggressively in low-income communities and took an increasing number of Pell-eligible students as transfers from community colleges—without apparent negative effect on the academic strength of its student body.[41]

If we step back from these particulars, what kind of general picture emerges? The stark truth is that America's colleges—with such notable exceptions as community colleges, historically black colleges, distinctive institutions such as Berea College in Kentucky (which charges no tuition and requires campus work from its students, all of whom are first in their families to attend college), along with a very few elite institutions with large endowments—have lately been reinforcing more than ameliorating the disparity of wealth and opportunity in American society. One writer goes so far as to call our leading colleges "propaganda machines that might as well have been designed to ensure that the class structure of American society remains unchallenged."[42]

Even if admissions policies were to change fundamentally at selective colleges, there will never be room for more than a fraction of the students worthy of going to them. Some of these colleges are expanding, but mostly with an eye toward admitting more students from abroad, who are often the children of the globetrotting business and political elite. Moreover, too many worthy students in today's America are unable to continue their education beyond high school at all—and of those who do, too many find themselves in colleges that are underfunded and overcrowded. "Over the last forty years," as one community college president writes, "enrollment in community colleges has expanded at a rate four times greater than in four-year public and private universities, yet they are able to expend only one third as much per full-time student as their better-financed private and public counterparts."[43] This means that the very students who most urgently need mentoring and support—first-generation college students, often minorities—are the ones who find reduced hours in the library and laboratory, cutbacks in advising, remedial tutoring, and child care, and who are likely to be taught by underpaid, overworked part-time faculty trying to cobble together a living by teaching at two or three campuses at the same time. It is hardly surprising that evidence of substantial learning is scant and that rates of graduation among many college students are low—especially in public institutions.[44]

One might expect this situation to elicit the kind of outrage we are quick to feel about the prejudices and privileges of the past. If anything, the obstacles that bright low-income students face today are more insidious than the frank exclusionary practices that once prevailed. On her application for a course that a colleague and I teach on this subject, one Columbia junior wrote about her friends who attended New York City public schools (she went to a Catholic high school in the South Bronx with good college counseling), that they "did not know when to apply for college, what forms they had to fill out or how to fill them out, let alone the name of a college outside the CUNY system."

And yet there seems to be much less indignation about the present than about the past, in part, perhaps, because as our society divides more and more between those with "advantages" (our euphemism for money) and those without, the two camps know less and less about each other. It's hard to know whom or what to hold accountable. Should we blame political or academic leaders, or maybe taxpayers—that convenient abstraction that includes ourselves? If we sat in the legislature, are we sure we'd cast the right vote when forced to allocate scarce funds between, say, Medicaid and higher education?[45] The hard fact is that in the absence of fundamental change in our tax structure and political priorities, the days of "both . . . and" are over, and the days of "either . . . or" have arrived.

FIVE

BRAVE NEW WORLD

Despite the unpalatable facts that I've just reviewed, the word often used today to describe people who succeed in getting into and through college, especially our most selective and prestigious colleges, is "meritocracy"—a name for those who get to the top because they are intelligent, hardworking, and ambitious. It's a word with an interesting genealogy. It sounds as if it were derived from the ancient Greek along with such words as "aristocracy" or "oligarchy," but in fact it is little more than fifty years old, coined in 1958 by an English social critic named Michael Young, who meant it not as an approving name for outstanding people but as a description of a nightmare social order that he feared was becoming reality.

Young's book, *The Rise of the Meritocracy*, was not a work of history. It was a futuristic fiction that imagined, from the vantage point of the year 2033, a gruesomely competitive society based on the formula "I + E = M" (intelligence plus effort equals merit), in which, by means of standardized testing starting early in childhood, the population is sorted into two main tracks: one, via elite educational institutions, toward wealth and power; the other, via apprenticeship or vocational training, toward relative penury and subservience. At the time, Young's fanciful future struck readers as outlandish (who would think of testing three-year-olds?!), but in fact his book belongs to the dark genre of prophetic fiction that includes Aldous Huxley's *Brave New World* (1932) with its dystopian vision of drug-induced pleasures, and Graham Greene's *The Quiet American* (1955), about the mix of idealism, innocence, and arrogance that draws the United States into unwinnable wars.

With Young's prescient book in mind, the historian Jerome Karabel has summed up the history of selective college admissions as "a history of recurrent struggles over the meaning of 'merit.'"[1] In this struggle, the winning faction always imposes its self-endorsing definition of merit on the losers. So naturally, in 1900, merit implied the haleness and heartiness of the "clubbable" man. Such a man didn't talk, or even think, much about money—in large part because he didn't have to. He drank, but not too much. He cultivated a personal style that's been called (in a variation on the title of Max Weber's famous book *The Protestant Ethic and the Spirit of Capitalism*) the "Protestant aesthetic." In the face of travail, he could be counted on to remain "outwardly indifferent, as all Anglo-Saxons" should be.[2] Women, of course, did not have this kind of merit. Catholics and Jews and blacks did not have it either.

But there was something else for which this meritorious man, in the ideal, at least, could be counted on. Despite his asperities and prejudices and blinkered view of the world, he was expected to have a concept of duty that extended beyond his own caste. Here is Charles W. Eliot's aspirational account of the "aristocracy" to which

the sons of Harvard have belonged, and, let us hope,
will ever aspire to belong—the aristocracy which excels
in manly sports, carries off the honors and prizes of the
learned professions, and bears itself with distinction in
all fields of intellectual labor and combat; the aristocracy
which in peace stands firmest for the public honor and re-
nown, and in war rides first into the murderous thickets.[3]

This sounds like brazen self-praise, and no doubt was more often stated in theory than observed in practice, but it does have
some historical warrant. The Harvard building, Memorial Hall,
in which Eliot's ninetieth birthday was celebrated, had been built
as a memorial to the nearly one hundred students and alumni,
at a time when the college numbered around five hundred, who
gave their lives in the Civil War, including many who did much
to turn it into a war against slavery. Another two hundred were
wounded. Perhaps best known among the dead was Robert
Gould Shaw (class of 1860), who left college early and went on to
lead a regiment of black volunteers into "the murderous thickets"
on an island off the coast of South Carolina, where he and virtually all his troops died in the assault on Fort Wagner.[4]

In *The Bostonians* (1886), Henry James gives a description
of Memorial Hall, through the vestibule of which students still
pass today into a dining hall on one side and a lecture hall on the
other. En route, they must walk past

white, ranged tablets, each of which, in its proud, sad
clearness, is inscribed with the name of a student-soldier.
The effect of the place is singularly noble and solemn, and
it is impossible to feel it without a lifting of the heart. It
stands there for duty and honour, it speaks of sacrifice
and example, seems a kind of temple to youth, manhood,

generosity. Most of them were young, all were in their prime, and all of them had fallen . . .[5]

It is not easy today to make out the names carved in the rows of white stone, which are mounted high on the wall and dimly lit, but it is impossible to see them, however indistinctly, without feeling how remote we are from the young men whom they memorialize. The closest to war that most of their counterparts come today is through stories of sit-ins and walk-outs that they've heard from their baby-boomer parents (now the senior faculty), whose war reminiscences begin and end, like mine, with how they avoided going to Vietnam. At leading American colleges outside the South, very few people—except for support and maintenance staff, who are much more likely to have family or friends in the line of fire—have experienced war. Perhaps the deepest divide in our country today runs between those for whom war is a relentless threat and those for whom it's an occasional television show. At our most prestigious colleges, the former is now the most underrepresented minority group.

No one, of course, should be held accountable for when or to whom they are born, and many academics would be quick to declare that some, if not most, of America's wars have been acts of jingoism or travesties of misguided idealism, and that honorable military service is an imperfect measure of merit. But apart from the test of war, to which history subjects some generations and not others, surely it is fair to ask about the condition of that more general sentiment we call civic duty. What is the record of the "meritocracy" in this regard?

There is a case to be made that for much of the twentieth century it was pretty good. What Henry James (who avoided the Civil War because of a "back injury") called "duty and honor" were high among the virtues that college was meant to encourage. They were, for instance, the themes of that best-selling novel *Stover at Yale*, which Scott Fitzgerald called "the textbook for my generation." A book more cited today than read, it is usually dismissed as a childish story about sons of the rich "punching" for the clubs at Old Eli, but in fact it is an account of a privileged insider coming to "a critical analysis of his own good fortune."[6] The Yale we meet in *Stover* is a place still tinged with its founders' belief that God dispenses grace by his inscrutable whim, and that those who find themselves smiled upon by God must live, when confronted by the suffering of others, with the humbling knowledge that "there but for the grace of God go I."

Yale exerts a force on Stover like that of a guilty dream. From its "misty walls and the elm-tops confounded in the night, a monstrous hand seemed to stretch down, impending over him" until the windows were "transformed into myriad eyes, set on him in inquisition." The eyes of Yale follow him everywhere, demanding that he subordinate himself to an "idea of sacrifice and self-abnegation."[7] No doubt many, if not most, of Stover's classmates flunked out of this idealized "school for character," and saw the world instead as Yale's well-known turn-of-the-century professor, the Social Darwinist William Graham Sumner, saw it—as a dog-eat-dog contest in which the fit prevail and the weak can go to hell. Sumner's best-known book bore the implicitly interrogative title *What Social Classes Owe to Each Other*, to which the implied answer was: not a damn thing.

Yet even if Sumner's was the real Yale, and Stover's Yale a myth, it was a good myth, and it helped to produce good men. One of the striking paradoxes in the history of elite colleges is that it was the sons of the old tribe who opened up their tribal institutions—not only colleges, but also corporations and clubs—to the larger world.

At Harvard, though there were periods of regression, the transformation advanced fairly steadily. At Princeton, which Woodrow Wilson envisioned as a "school of duty," it was much slower—as was Wilson himself on matters of what today we would call race and class, not to mention gender. At Yale, the change took place rather suddenly under the presidency of Kingman Brewster (Mayflower descendant, Yale '41, president from 1963 to 1977), when the numbers of black students rose substantially and women were admitted for the first time. The same progressive spirit was carried beyond New Haven by a number of Brewster's fellow patricians, notably the industrialist and philanthropist J. Irwin Miller (Yale, '31), a pioneer in promoting racial integration in the business world, and Paul Moore (Yale, '41), Episcopal bishop of New York, who turned the Cathedral of St. John the Divine from a high WASP enclave in upper Manhattan into an ecumenical institution serving the community of Harlem.

These men—along with near contemporaries such as Cyrus Vance ('39), Sargent Shriver ('38), John Lindsay ('44), and William Sloane Coffin ('49)—recognized their own privilege as blind luck at best or injustice at worst. Narrow old Yale was destroyed by large-minded old Yalies. And every elite institution has had its own version of the loyal opposition, though it has been stronger at some than at others.[8] Clark Kerr, who created the world's most open system of public higher education, went to a small private college, Swarthmore, certainly among the most elite (as measured by its intellectual standards) colleges in the United States.

2

Dropping in on the world of the old meritocracy can be a useful exercise for gaining perspective on what college worthiness means today. Perhaps the most vivid representative of the old order was a half-fictional figure named Frank Prescott, the title character of *The Rector of Justin* (1964), Louis Auchincloss's novel about a prep-school headmaster loosely modeled on Endicott Peabody, the renowned headmaster of Groton School from 1884 till 1940—though the fictional Prescott is less religious than was the actual Peabody. Prescott-Peabody grew up at a time when a gentleman would not offer a lady a chair in which someone had recently been sitting, since there is "nothing more horrid than a warm seat."[9] Today, we can hardly believe such people existed. But Prescott is no prude; he detests snobbery, and holds an unsentimental view of war, while insisting that those who are first in line for peacetime privilege must also be first to step up in wartime. Above all, he thinks that the point of education is to inspire people to public service.

To this end, he has a view of what teaching ought to be. "The older I get," he tells a younger member of the school faculty, "the more I realize that the only thing a teacher has to go on is that rare spark in a boy's eye. And when you see *that* . . . you're an ass if you worry where it comes from. Whether it's an ode of Horace, or an Icelandic Saga, or something that goes bang in a laboratory."[10] These are examples of what William James called "invasive experiences" capable of "abruptly upsetting the equilibrium of the primary consciousness"—and whether such an experience comes via the study of nature (the bang in the lab), or music, or art, or mathematics, or the involuntary selflessness to which one is lifted by examples of virtue in literature or history or life, it is asinine to worry where it comes from. The only thing that matters is what it leads to—or what James, paraphrasing St. Paul, called its "fruits for life."

Measured by this standard, a good many members of the old "meritocracy" lived their lives well. Franklin Roosevelt (Groton, class of 1900, Harvard '04), who revered Peabody, was by no means a brilliant student, but because of school and family he was assured of going to Harvard whether he spent his summers playing polo or working as a camp counselor for poor urban children. (He did both, and this was before the age of padding resumés with evidence of altruism.) Upon first meeting Roosevelt, Justice Oliver Wendell Holmes (Harvard, class of 1861, thrice-wounded Civil War veteran) remarked that the new president seemed a man with a "second rate mind but a first-class temperament." At most elite-college admissions offices today such an assessment would cut no ice—probably not even if the candidate is backed by old money.

Is there a challenge in this alien past to our present criteria of membership in the "meritocracy"? What should we make of the fact that Roosevelt and his team of Ivy advisors—old boys, almost to a man—did more than most people with advantages do to foster hope for the disadvantaged? When Social Security got through Congress, Peabody wrote to his former student to praise him for acting on the conviction "that there should be throughout the land a great emphasis laid upon the duty of the citizen to the community and this even among those who were formerly considering only their own interests."[11] How do today's best and brightest stack up?

It is, of course, a loaded question—utterly unfair, tainted by the sort of "Greatest Generation" nostalgia in which Americans have lately indulged, and based on the dubious premise that one can generalize usefully about any generation, however we choose to define that vague term. Such a question is not susceptible to a verifiable answer, since people are, in part, products of their times and, except in some time-travel fantasy, can't be lifted out of history and dropped into some other time. But when it was asked of me some fifteen years ago, it provoked me to think about college in a way I had not thought of before.

It came in the form of a rhetorical question, at the Rittenhouse Hotel in Philadelphia, where I had the good fortune of meeting over breakfast with E. Digby Baltzell, the man often credited with popularizing the term "The Establishment." Born to an upper-crust Philadelphia family, Baltzell stayed home for college at Penn rather than going off to Harvard because his family had fallen on hard times. After college, he served as a navy pilot in World War II, took a PhD at Columbia under Robert Merton (the child of Jewish immigrants, born, also in Philadelphia, under the name Meyer Schkolnik), then went on to write extensively about the American social elite in such works as his well-known book *The Protestant Establishment: Aristocracy and Caste in America* (1964).

He was the very picture of the old boy. He wore a herringbone jacket slightly on the loud side, a rosy shirt with a touch of starch, his hair brushed back in the windswept style of a sailing man. After we sat down, he leaned back and, without pausing for preliminary niceties, asked, "So where did you go to college?" "Harvard," I said, with no idea where this was going. And then came the challenging question: "Do you think you deserved to go there?" This was a stumper. I hemmed and hawed—not sure whether to prevaricate with something like, not really, there were brighter kids in my high school who could have made more of the opportunity. Or should I say what he knew I was thinking: yes, why not, I worked hard, got good grades, have done nicely in my chosen work ever since? He didn't wait for an answer. "Of course you do!" he said, and followed with this indictment: "You and your whole generation are the smuggest, most self-satisfied in the history of the republic. You figured you had earned what you got, whereas when Jack Kennedy went to Harvard, he knew he was there because of his daddy's money—and when he got out, he felt he ought to give something back!" It was all said with a smile, but also with a hint of anger.

This was doubtless a romanticized view of the young JFK, but the larger point was a forceful one. As I later understood when I came to read *The Rise of the Meritocracy*, it was, in essence, Michael Young's point. What Young and Baltzell were talking about was the Anglo-American version of *noblesse oblige*—a conception that seems much attenuated now that "merit has become progressively more measurable."[12] In our era of social sorting by academic prowess, which Young placed in an imaginary future but which we know firsthand, the "new upper classes are no longer weakened by self-doubt and self-criticism," and, all too often, subscribe to "the axiom of modern thought . . . that people are unequal, and . . . that they should be accorded a station in life related to their capacities."[13]

It is hard not to be fortified in this view as one goes through today's college admissions process, which effectively begins in preschool (with, yes, the testing of three-year-olds), accelerates through childhood, consumes much of adolescence, and comes to a climax on the cusp of adulthood. This series of trials and rewards is well designed to convince the winners that they deserve their winnings—a conviction in which new freshmen are encouraged when the college president welcomes them with some version of the standard accolade: "You are the most extraordinary class ever to walk through our gates." When Young spoke of being "weakened . . . by self-criticism," he spoke ironically, of course, since he counted self-doubt and self-criticism among the virtues of a genuinely educated person—though he certainly did not think that such virtues are limited to people with educational credentials. "Today," as he put it with tart irony, "the eminent know that success is just reward for their own capacity, for their own efforts, and for their own undeniable achievement," and "become so impressed with their own importance as to lose sympathy with the people whom they govern."[14]

The Rise of the Meritocracy was an amazingly astute description of what we have become—a society "dedicated to the one overriding purpose of economic expansion," in which "people are judged according to the single test of how much they increase production." In such a society, "the scientist whose invention does the work of ten thousand, or the administrator who organizes clutches of technicians" is counted "among the great," and intelligence is defined as "the ability to raise production, directly or indirectly."[15] It's a definition that makes things dicey for those whom Young, with devilish delight, called "IQ berserkers," by which he meant those "with an I.Q. of 140 at some times and 90 at others, and not only when in love or before breakfast." Among Young's accurate prophecies was that "a beneficent by-product of educational selection," would be therapies by which the mind could be focused and mood swings smoothed out.[16]

The bracingly polemical writer Walter Benn Michaels has carried Young's analysis of the putatively meritocratic society into the context of contemporary America. Our leading colleges, he says, "have become our primary mechanism for convincing ourselves that poor people deserve their poverty," and that if you're rich, you got that way "because you're better."[17] Few people inside or outside academia would say such a thing openly, at least not without softening it with protestations of humility, but the fact is that many people secretly—or not so secretly—believe it.[18]

The new meritocracy, of course, has gone global. The ranklist mania seems even more manic in Asia, where Shanghai University now sponsors a widely followed academic ranking that calculates institutional quality on the basis of such measures as numbers of Nobel prizes and Fields medals (a prestigious international award in mathematics) won by the faculty, as well as the number of faculty publications in such journals as *Science* and *Nature*. There are no measures pertinent to the liberal education of undergraduates. It is hard to know how there could be.

Those who don't stand high on these lists are indignant. The director of the École normale supérieure—the premiere postsecondary institution in France—is unhappy about how the École fared (it came in twenty-eighth out of two hundred world universities in the *Times* (of London) *Higher Education* rankings a couple of years ago, and seventy-third in the Shanghai contest). She protests by explaining what it takes for students to get into the École: "the competition between students is such that one who succeeds by the end of *classes préparatoires* would have typically studied for twelve to sixteen hours a day without holiday for two or three years."[19] In India, it is not unusual for ambitious high school students to leave home to live in "coaching centers" where they work all day every day at improving their exam-taking skills since everything depends on their performance on the Indian Institutes of Technology Joint Entrance Exam (IIT-JEE).[20] In China, roughly ten million high school students take an exam hoping to snare one of the roughly six million places in college. Are these really the people we want running the world? Sleep-deprived, ruthlessly competitive, type AAA personalities, driven to the edge of endurance?

Of course it is one thing to recoil from the present or worry about the future, and quite another to glorify the past, which won't stand up to too much scrutiny either. There has never been any shortage of hypocrisy, fakery, posturing, and downright silliness in America's colleges, including—perhaps especially—the leading colleges. A few months after Robert Gould Shaw died in the assault on Fort Wagner, Julian Hawthorne (Harvard, class of 1868) capped off his freshman year of "rodomontade and horseplay" by spending the night in a coffin as part of a drunken hazing ritual—the same night, grotesquely enough, that his father, Nathaniel Hawthorne, died.[21] (Late in life, Julian Hawthorne spent a year in federal prison on a mail fraud charge.) Perhaps most college men, to use William Perry's formulation, have always been "schoolboys." It may be ridiculous to idealize and universalize, say, the "tall, blonde, lean, and wasp-waisted" William Francis Bartlett (Harvard, class of 1862), who, unlike Shaw, survived the war and came back, one-legged, to be celebrated in poetry by Herman Melville as having "lived a thousand years / Compressed in battle's pains and prayers."[22] But it's not ridiculous to note that such men had—or made— opportunities to discover for themselves certain principles that too many elite colleges now seem to discount: that courage and selflessness are democratically distributed virtues (something, I believe, that many people learn in war), and that with privilege comes responsibility.

If it's easy to romanticize the past, it is harder to make the case that these principles are alive and well in the "best" colleges of the present. In the context of the story I have tried to tell, another way to put the matter is to say that some of these colleges have now arrived at a conception of themselves that is the reverse of where they began. Notably, in an age when bipartisan consensus is hard to come by, this is a point on which left and right cordially agree. For the left-liberal Walter Benn Michaels, elite colleges are in the business of building up the self-love of their students by "legitimizing their sense of their individual merit."

For Ross Douthat, a conservative writer who has since become a *New York Times* columnist,

> ruling classes have always believed in their own right to rule, but it once was understood—at least by anyone who cared to think seriously about the matter—that their place in the social order was arbitrary, an accident of birth and breeding, rather than a matter of cosmic justice. Ideals of noblesse oblige grew from just this sense: the knowledge that God (or blind chance) had given the elite much that was not necessarily deserved.

Today, however,

> that knowledge has been wiped away. The modern elite's rule is regarded not as arbitrary but as just and right and true, at least if one follows the logic of meritocracy to its unspoken conclusion . . . [today's elite] belong exactly where they are—the standardized tests and the college admissions officers have spoken, and their word is final.[23]

The shared point here is that our oldest colleges have abandoned the cardinal principle of the religion out of which they arose: the principle that no human being deserves anything based on his or her merit. In that view—too harsh, perhaps, for anyone except a saint to live by—when God announced to Abraham that he had chosen him for an exalted role in history, he did so "without any respect unto any goodness in Abraham," but rather "freely of his grace . . . for it is nothing God seeth in Abraham, for which he doth reveal his justification to him."[24] Such a God was not impressed by any demonstration of meritorious behavior in any human being. To the extent that human beings are capable of worthy actions, they are unmerited gifts from a merciful God, and should be occasions for humility rather than pride.

So it was appropriate that Jerome Karabel gave a title with a biblical ring, *The Chosen*, to his history of how the eastern elite lost its grip on their beloved Harvard, Yale, and Princeton. He tells in that book a story of progress, and rightly points out that few people would deny that "the quasi-meritocratic admissions system of today is a major improvement over the more overtly discriminatory and hereditary system of the past." And yet he concludes with a call "to heed Young's final warning"—that "we neglect the dark side of our meritocracy at our collective peril."[25]

3

A number of writers have lately taken us on a tour of the dark side. Among the liveliest is Walter Kirn, who, in an alternately hilarious and harrowing memoir, *Lost in the Meritocracy : The Education of an Overachiever* (2009), sums up his Princeton classmates (he was graduated in 1983) in the figure of "the mental contortionist, able to rise to almost every challenge placed before him at school or work except, perhaps, to the challenge of real self-knowledge."[26] It is hard to write this way and stay on the right side of decency, since any such report on one's peers begins as an act of espionage under the cover of friendship, and there is a certain pettiness in blaming youth culture on the young. College students have always run the full range from seekers to fakers, and while every college teacher encounters students who are crass and grasping, he or she also knows others who are ingenuous, curious, and wonderfully free of self-delight. It's a mixed picture, as any honest portrait of individuals or institutions must be. Yet Kirn is right to ask if our educational institutions couldn't be doing more today to save us from ourselves. I use the inclusive "us" because we were all young once, and because the young will soon be old.

A quick survey of what might be called the ethical landscape of today's colleges may give an idea of how much work remains to be done—starting at the top. For one thing, many colleges, especially those high in the pecking order, have gotten much too close to the world of money. Nineteenth-century Harvard impressed Charles Dickens as a place where "the almighty dollar sinks into something comparatively insignificant, amidst a whole Pantheon of better gods." Today it is common for leaders of top colleges to garnish their presidential pay (seven figures are no longer unheard of) by sitting on highly remunerative corporate boards. The president of Rensselaer Polytechnic Institute sits on the boards of Fedex, Marathon Oil, and IBM (among others), handsomely supplementing her annual salary of nearly $2 million—though it should be noted that these numbers pale beside the earnings of for-profit "university" CEOs, such as the president of Strayer University, who took home $43 million last year. Meanwhile, the leaders of Stanford and Princeton catch up with each other at board meetings of Google, and the chancellor of the University of Illinois at Urbana-Champaign sits on the board of Nike, which holds a contract with the university for supplying athletic shirts adorned with the Nike swoosh. At worst, this sort of thing is a conflict of interest; at best it is unseemly. When, in the wake of the financial contraction of 2008–2009, Tufts president Lawrence Bacow declined to be paid as much as the trustees proposed to pay him, he was setting an all-too-rare example of a leader who takes seriously "the symbolic importance of president's salaries," especially in times of retrenchment.[27]

What about the faculty? Outside the elite reaches of academia, many college teachers are underpaid and overworked, devoted to their students at cost to themselves. But they tend to be obscured in the public eye by their more visible counterparts: media-star professors who jet around the globe from Aspen to Davos, chatter on TV, and provide more prestige than time to their home institutions. In his dean's report to the Harvard faculty twenty years ago, Henry Rosovsky wrote that it had become "a society largely without rules, or to put it slightly differently, the tenured members of the faculty—frequently as *individuals*—make their own rules" with regard to teaching loads, outside business ventures, consulting time versus teaching time, and so on. A me-first ethos, Rosovsky said, was destroying what was left of an older civic attitude according to which "a professor's primary obligation is to the institution—essentially students and colleagues—and that all else is secondary." Five years later, in a book entitled *Academic Duty* (1997), Donald Kennedy, former president of Stanford, made a laudable effort to clarify the responsibilities that ought to go hand in hand with academic freedom. Unfortunately, this sort of critique, accurate and salutary as it may be, can also give aid and comfort to those who charge the whole professoriate with selfishness and self-indulgence.

One reason for public suspicion is that moneymaking opportunities for well-placed academics (particularly, but by no means only, in the sciences), as well as for the institutions where they work, have jumped because of growth in "technology-transfer" partnerships with corporate investors and government agencies. This has been especially true since 1980, when Congress passed the Bayh-Dole Act permitting institutions and individuals to share in profits from inventions or therapies developed with public funds. And if the boundary between "pure" and "applied" research is no longer much observed, neither is the line between consultation and collaboration. Many leading academic economists who have held public office have close ties to investment or insurance firms that are subject to the regulatory and tax policies these same economists help to formulate. And it's not just the Washington–Wall Street highway that's clogged with commuting professors. In the run-up to war in Libya, it became known that a group of prominent political scientists, sociologists, and professors of business was collecting hundreds of thousands of dollars per month from the Qaddafi government in return for "consulting" services. One of the beneficiaries wrote favorable op-ed articles about Colonel Qaddafi's sincere commitment to democratization—without bothering to disclose his financial relation to the Libyan regime.[28]

And what about the students? Most don't lead pampered lives of self-indulgence—far from it—but, as with faculty, the gap is widening between the majority and the select few. Nearly 150 years ago, when Charles W. Eliot remarked that "luxury and learning are ill bed fellows," the phrase was a commonplace expressing a consensus across a broad range of institutions. Today, top colleges vie for students by offering amenities superior to those of the competition—better-stocked coffee bars in the library, better-equipped fitness centers in the dorms, and so on. At some colleges, the campus tour now resembles a promotional tour of a luxury resort. In 1900, one observer of college life remarked that "it makes a great difference" if a young person spends the years between eighteen and twenty-two "in a counting house, where the clocks measure nothing but interest, and where . . . he [must] master this grim and terrible religion of money, or whether these years shall be spent amid surroundings that may awaken the youth to a noble ambition." Today, the tone of college life can be gleaned by glancing at some representative titles of recent books: *Saving Higher Education in the Age of*

Money; Universities in the Marketplace: The Commercialization of Higher Education; Shakespeare, Einstein and the Bottom Line: The Marketing of Higher Education; University, Inc.: The Corporate Corruption of Higher Education—to name just a few. One Ivy League dean recently declared that universities should simply give up the fantasy of holding to academic values that stand apart from the culture of "universal commodification."[29]

This attitude, somewhere between realism and cynicism, surrenders much of what has been most valuable in the history of our colleges and universities: their deliberate distance from the world of getting and spending in which young people are destined to spend so much of their lives. Before the crash of 2008, with the money chase totally out of control, a few academic leaders did try to point out the cost—moral, psychological, social—of giving in to the commodification of everything. Soon after taking office as Harvard's president in the winter of 2007, Drew Faust challenged the first graduating class to which she spoke at commencement to reflect on why nearly 60 percent of men in the previous year's class and over 40 percent of women took jobs in what is euphemistically called "financial services." Five years later, the illusions of those days, when young people fresh out of top colleges lived "in the cheerful expectation that sooner or later a bolt of pecuniary fire would jump out of the atmosphere and knock you flat," may be scarcer and weaker.[30] But the fire is starting to burn again, and those colleges where it burns the brightest are at least as much bastions of privilege as they ever were in the age of the old "meritocracy." In fact, for reasons discussed in the last chapter, they are probably more so.

Today's colleges also have some obvious problems with integrity and civility. At Tom Wolfe's fictional "Dupont University" (apparently based on Duke), students like to greet each other with salutations like "fucking ape-faced dickhead." This image of the profane and promiscuous student, like that of the jet-set professor, is a caricature—indeed, a slander—of the great many students who, under unrelenting social as well as academic stress, take college seriously and try to make the best of their opportunities. Many opt out of the hypersexualized atmosphere that prevails on some campuses. Many work diligently, and honestly, with an appetite for learning as well as for success. Still, like any caricature, Wolfe's version of college life as a frantic chase after pleasure and power is not without an element of truth.

For one thing, cheating, especially in the form of plagiarism, is rampant—not just at "Dupont" but everywhere. A few years ago, the *New York Times* reported that "students are fuzzy on what's cheating and what's not," while people outside the universities looking to cash in on the putative confusion are not the least bit fuzzy about how to do so. Among the many websites offering term papers for sale, one has the winningly candid name CheatHouse.com. I know two faculty friends at a prestigious college who entertain themselves each spring at the commencement ceremony by going through the printed program checking off names of seniors whom they know to have submitted at least one plagiarized paper. It's not uncommon for these students to be graduating with honors.

None of this, of course, is new. Former Columbia College dean Robert Pollack, a biologist, tells the story of the organic chemistry lab in which he was enrolled as an undergraduate in 1961. Hoping to get an A on the assignment to synthesize acetylsalicylic acid, premeds "in a hurry" bought some aspirin at the local drugstore, ground it up, and submitted a pure white powder in their test tubes that compared favorably to everyone else's brown sludge. Unaware that the TAs had spiked the starting material with a radioactive marker, all the cheaters were caught by a simple Geiger-counter test. So academic dishonesty has always been a problem—but it's squeamish to pretend that things have not gotten worse.[31]

Some people believe that a main contributor to the sorry state of academic ethics, especially to the contagion of money, is what Andrew Hacker and Claudia Dreifus, in their recent book *Higher Education? How Colleges Are Wasting Our Money and Failing Our Kids—and What We Can Do About It*, call the "athletic incubus." This charge has some basis in a national context where football coaches, sometimes paid in the millions, collude with administrators to provide fake credits for courses never taken, and strippers and prostitutes are hired to show a good time to recruits who, once they've arrived on campus, sign up for courses on "Coaching Principles and Strategies of Basketball," with exam questions such as "How Many Halves are in a Basketball Game?" It all sounds straight out of *MAD* magazine, but such practices are well documented. Like academic dishonesty, corruption in college athletics is hardly new. In 1951, at City College—renowned for its high standards—four basketball players were charged with shaving points in collusion with local gamblers. "You bribed them to play for you," one journalist wrote about the college. "The gamblers paid them not to play too well. What's the difference?"[32]

To be sure, such abuses are less egregious at institutions that forbid athletic scholarships in the sense of funds targeted for desired recruits regardless of need, and where revenues from ticket sales, licensing, and television contracts pale by comparison to those where sports are big business. Problems—exploiting student-athletes, then discarding them if their on-field performance disappoints; not to mention the mind-boggling sexual abuse scandal at Penn State—tend to be worst in high-stakes programs. Yet it should be noted that athletes account for a higher percentage of students in the Ivy League than in the Big Ten, and are a main reason that even after they had putatively abandoned early admission programs, Harvard and Princeton continued to send out hundreds of "likely admit" letters to varsity prospects months before most other applicants knew their fate. In the Ivies, financial incentives beyond demonstrated need are not permitted for recruiting any applicant— athletic or otherwise—but a significant number (typically around 20 percent) of places in the class are, to all intents and purposes, reserved for recruits needed to fill the team rosters. Other highly selective institutions, too, make academic compromises to meet athletic imperatives. At Stanford, where athletic scholarships are permitted, a "Courses of Interest" list—including "Beginning Improvising" and "Social Dances of North America"—was provided to athletes until the *Chronicle of Higher Education* broke the story and the university, embarrassed, discontinued the list.[33]

The fact is that at virtually every residential college today, competitive athletic (as opposed to physical fitness) facilities rank high on the list of fund-raising priorities, and no president would be caught saying, as one said in the early days of varsity sports, "I will not permit thirty men to travel four hundred miles merely to agitate a bag of wind"—by which he meant a football, not a professor. Deploying statistics that show inferior academic performance by recruited athletes at all types of colleges, William Bowen has long argued that "college sports in their current form represent a distinct threat to academic values and educational excellence." Former Harvard College dean Harry Lewis, however, celebrates college athletes as prodigies living alongside their classmates in "a glorious parallel universe . . . detached from the banality of ordinary life."[34] There is truth in both views. Anyone who has taught in any college has encountered some student-athletes who, unprepared for college work, are bewildered and exploited, while others are disciplined students, grateful for the opportunity their physical gifts have helped them to earn, and eager, as the phrase goes, to "give back." This doesn't stop many on campus, students and faculty alike, from deriding "jocks" with a contempt that would never be tolerated if aimed at any other group.

Today, as always, generalizing about college students is a risky business. A few years ago, I was invited to participate in a discussion on "Religion in a Pluralist Society," to be convened at Columbia by a student group called the "Veritas Forum," with which I was unfamiliar. Upon learning that this organization defines its mission as engaging "students and faculty in discussions about life's hardest questions and the relevance of Jesus Christ to all of life," I was, as a (nonobservant) Jew, a little puzzled, and expected a sparse turnout on a campus not exactly known for its evangelical fervor. In fact, the largest lecture hall in the university was packed, and those present impressed me with their combination of high moral seriousness and intellectual curiosity. We tend to think of universities, especially elite ones, as bastions of skepticism toward all things religious, but this is a partial view at best. In the prevailing typology of the contemporary academy, many of the students in the room that evening would have been categorized as "Asian American"—although, as the event proceeded, it became clear that they were more likely to think of themselves in the first instance as Christians.

In short, a truthful tour of today's colleges would leave the open-minded tourist with few preconceptions intact. It would be a trip neither to the dark side nor to a world of bright ideals. Why would it be? Colleges are no more independent of the larger culture than any other institution; they "contain multitudes," as Walt Whitman said of himself, from honor to perfidy, from vulgarity to refinement, and everything in between. For every student squandering time, others are making the best of their college years not only in academic work but, one way or another, in service to their community.

Yet one generalization, I think, applies across the board: there is a sense of drift. Before the financial crash, students were fleeing from "useless" subjects such as literature or the arts, and flocking to "marketable" subjects such as economics. Now, in the lingering aftermath of the global financial crisis, the flight continues; many students are also wondering what, in fact, is useful for what. Even at elite institutions, one feels more than a hint of panic about postcollege life. Young people know that time-tested assumptions about the best route to this or that vocation, about how to find a mate and satisfying work, how to prosper and save, how to balance needs with wants—in short, how to make a life—are being called into radical doubt.

Unfortunately, by failing to reconnect their students to the idea that good fortune confers a responsibility to live generously toward the less fortunate, too many colleges are doing too little to help students cope with this siege of uncertainty. One of the insights at the core of the college idea—indeed of the idea of community itself—has always been that to serve others is to serve oneself by providing a sense of purpose, thereby countering the loneliness and aimlessness by which all people, young and old, can be afflicted. Yet, as Christopher Jencks and David Riesman pointed out more than forty years ago, in the professionalized academy, "moral and political questions that cannot be resolved by research and do not yield to cooperative investigation are almost by definition outside the academic orbit."[35] In the last few decades we have seen the rise of compensatory institutions within the institutions, such as the Center for Human Values at Princeton, or the Institute for Ethics at Duke. But what does it mean that thinking about ethics has become an extracurricular activity?

In a book aptly titled *Universities in the Marketplace* (2003), former Harvard president Derek Bok more or less repeated Jencks and Riesman's observation when he wrote that "faculties currently display scant interest in preparing undergraduates to be democratic citizens, a task once regarded as the principal purpose of a liberal education and one urgently needed at this moment in the United States."[36] Perhaps it's because it was such old news that he put it in a footnote.

SIX

WHAT IS TO BE DONE?

I have tried in this book to tell a story of ideas and institutions while keeping people—students, teachers, academic leaders—at the forefront of the tale. I did not want to stick to any one of the genres to which such a story usually conforms—jeremiad (invoking the past to shame the present), elegy (gone are the greats of yesteryear), call to arms (do this or that and we will be saved)—so the result, no doubt, is a messy mixture of them all.

In fact, if there is one form to which most recent writing about college belongs, it is none of the above, but, rather, the funeral dirge. Here's an example that appeared in the *Washington Post* soon after the economic meltdown whose consequences we are still trying to fathom:

> Students starting school this year [2009–10] may be part of the last generation for which "going to college" means packing up, getting a dorm room and listening to tenured professors. Undergraduate education is on the verge of a

radical reordering. Colleges, like newspapers, will be torn apart by new ways of sharing information enabled by the internet. The business model that sustained private U.S. colleges cannot survive.[1]

One benefit of looking into the past is to be reminded that apocalyptic prophecies are more often wrong than right. But in some respects this one has already come true.

By this I mean that the theme I've stressed—college as a community of learning—is, for many students, already an anachronism. If we count as liberal arts colleges the roughly six hundred institutions that make up the Council of Independent Colleges (an organization that does not include colleges within research universities), their total enrollment represents around one in fourteen of the nation's undergraduate students.[2] A couple of summers ago, in one of those reflective editorials that seeks to capture the mood of the season, the *New York Times* reported that "all across the country, poignantly overstuffed vehicles will be heading down the highway to campuses that will soon be turning autumnal."[3] What the *Times* failed to mention is that for every one of those college-bound cars, there are scores of families whose children will be staying home to attend a commuter school without anything resembling traditional college life.[4]

Moreover, millions of college-age Americans never get to college in the first place. For young people in our country whose families are in the bottom income quartile, the chance of going to college is about one in five. By the age of twenty-six, fewer than two-thirds of white high school graduates have enrolled in college, while for minorities the figure is significantly lower— slightly more than half for blacks and, for Hispanics, slightly less.

Among all students who do manage to enroll, roughly half finish at a different college from where they began, fewer than 60 percent finish within six years, and more than a third never finish at all.[5]

Yet college myths and memories have long been an important part of America's sense of what young adulthood is all about. Consider *The Big Chill*, or even that dubious classic *Animal House*. Think of the fictional Ron Patimkin swooning to his treasured LP of Ohio State school songs, "Goodbye, Columbus," in Philip Roth's novella of the same name, or this little recitative from the Broadway show *Avenue Q*:

> KATE MONSTER: I wish I could go back to college.
> Life was so simple back then.
> NICKY: What would I give to go back and live in a dorm
> with a meal plan again!
> PRINCETON: I wish I could go back to college.
> In college you know who you are.
> You sit in the quad, and think, "Oh my God!
> I am totally gonna go far!" . . .
> I wanna go back to my room and find a message in dry-
> erase pen on the door!
> Ohhh . . .
> I wish I could just drop a class . . .
> NICKY: Or get into a play . . .
> KATE MONSTER: Or change my major . . .
> PRINCETON: Or fuck my T.A. . . .
> NICKY: But if I were to go back to college,
> Think what a loser I'd be—
> I'd walk through the quad,
> And think "Oh my God . . . "
> ALL: "These kids are so much younger than me."

Perhaps, as this skit reminds us, our brains are programmed to edit out the failures and disappointments—the botched exams, missed free throws, unrequited loves—that can make college a difficult time for young people struggling to grow up.

If most students no longer have anything like the "traditional" college experience, neither do the people who teach them. In 1975, nearly 60 percent of college professors were full-time faculty with tenure or on the "tenure track." Today that fraction has declined to around 35 percent, which means that most students are being taught by part-time or contingent employees who have limited stake in the institution where they work.[6] Some highly regarded colleges play a game of what Berkeley professor David Kirp calls "bait and switch" by luring students with big-name faculty and then assigning them to classes taught by overworked part-timers.[7] These teachers—often excellent people forced to cobble together a subsistence wage by working in one college for part of the week, then in another (or others) for the rest of the week—have no assurance that they will be teaching next year at all. The author of a grimly entitled book, *The Last Professors*, plausibly describes this "dismantling of the American professoriate" as "part and parcel of the casualization of labor" that is under way throughout American life, along with the rise of outsourcing and the decline of unions.[8]

This vision of the imminent future remains a long way from realization at the old and prestigious colleges that have been at the center of this book. In fact, their appeal seems likely to grow precisely because they have the wealth and "market share" to retain a stable faculty teaching what they like, as they like. But at many other colleges, it is uncomfortably close to a description of how things already are. The professor shaping a course around his interests and sensibility (now known as the "independent-operator professor")[9] is becoming a relic, while the instructor-for-hire, whose job is to monitor standardized content over some "delivery system," is becoming the new norm. If she doesn't like the template of the course for which she has been hired, the institution will have no trouble hiring somebody else. By the rules of the marketplace—efficiency, cost effectiveness, and, for a growing number of institutions, profitability—it all makes sense. By the measures of educational value as I have defined it in this book, it makes no sense at all.

Even the wealthiest private colleges now find themselves straining for the resources they need (or think they need), while public institutions are reeling from the loss of tax revenues on which they still depend. Independent colleges are raising tuition to prohibitive levels and cutting back, sometimes without public acknowledgment, on financial aid. Community colleges— portals of opportunity for students from low-income and immigrant families (some 60 percent of Hispanic college students attend a community college)—are overwhelmed not only by students of traditional college age but also by adults hoping to learn skills that will help them find employment in a dire job market. Meanwhile, some private institutions that lack the allure of high prestige are finding it hard to meet their enrollment targets as prospective students choose a more affordable four-year public or two-year community college instead. As for the fastest-growing sector in higher education—the for-profit institutions—they provide, at best, narrow training in vocational subjects such as accounting or information technology. At worst, they take money in exchange for worthless credentials.[10]

In this new context, and in the face of disturbing evidence of poor student achievement—according to one recent study, roughly a quarter of college graduates cannot comprehend a moderately sophisticated magazine article, or estimate if there's enough gas in the car to reach the next gas station—a national movement has been forming to devise credible ways to assess what students are actually learning and to improve their prospects of learning more. Our current method of assessing college teachers—mainly surveying students about how much they like or dislike them—is atomistic, impressionistic, and generally close to worthless. "I have seen students fill a lecture room for the mere sake of entertainment," one professor wrote nearly two hundred years ago, "because the Professor interspersed his lecture (by no means the best of the university) with entertaining anecdotes."[11] At a time when faculty retention and promotion depend at least partly on student evaluations, the risk of this sort of thing is higher than ever.

As for evaluating the students themselves, grade inflation (also encouraged by student surveys, since few students appreciate a low grade) has at least kept pace with, if not exceeded, the epidemic of cheating. Except in the hard sciences, grades mean less and less, especially in elite colleges, where the numbers of students graduating with honors and with GPAs *over* 4.0 (the A+ is no longer uncommon) have become outlandish. What exactly a college degree signifies is now so variable across institutions, and, for that matter, within the same institution, that having the degree doesn't mean much either—leaving it at risk of becoming what one writer long ago called a "merely formal and unmeaning certificate."[12]

Meanwhile, American academic leaders, long accustomed to assuming that their institutions are without peer abroad, are looking nervously over their collective shoulder at the rising universities abroad, especially in China, as well as at "the Bologna process"—the movement in Europe to make degree requirements sufficiently compatible across national borders so that, for example, a baccalaureate in chemistry earned in a French university will be a portable credential qualifying the holder for further study or skilled employment, in, say, Belgium. In some countries, notably China and Germany, national civil service examinations were once used to assess what university students had learned—a past practice that may yet prove a model for the future.

2

There is no American counterpart to these traditions. In the late nineteenth century, when James McCosh argued for a relatively uniform undergraduate curriculum against Charles W. Eliot's proposal of free electives and relaxed attendance requirements, he made his case partly by comparing what America lacked with what Europe possessed:

> I know that in Germany they produce scholars without requiring a rigid attendance, and I rather think that in a few American colleges, they are aping this German method, thinking to produce equally diligent students. They forget that the Germans have one powerful safeguard which we have not in America. For all offices in Church and State there is an examination by high scholars following the college course. A young man cannot get an office as clergyman, as teacher, as postmaster, till he is passed by that terrible examining bureau, and if he is turned down by them his prospects in life are blasted. Let the State of Massachusetts pass a law like the Prussian, and Harvard may then relax attendance, and the State will do what the colleges have neglected to do.[13]

McCosh's point was that if colleges don't keep their houses in order, the state will—or should—do it for them.

Since then, at the secondary school level, Americans have become used to a testing regime that is administered privately (the

SAT, the ACT) or publicly (for example, the New York State Regents exam). Under President George W. Bush, the "No Child Left Behind" law attempted to strengthen that regime and hold schools and teachers accountable for the test scores of their students. But there is mounting evidence that the law has had little positive effect, and some say it has a negative effect by encouraging states to "dumb down" the tests, and by driving "soft" subjects such as art and music to the margins, or out of the curriculum altogether.[14] For most educators, the specter of government intrusion only threatens to introduce blunter instruments than those we already use for measuring what students learn.

It seems unlikely that such a regime will extend to our colleges anytime soon, but as a prod to action by colleges themselves, the prospect may actually be salutary. One distinctive aspect of American higher education has always been its decentralization: except for submitting to periodic accreditation reviews, colleges and universities enjoy virtually untrammeled freedom to conduct education as they see fit. On the other hand, very few colleges can be said to be strictly private in the sense of being accountable only to themselves. Ever since the Massachusetts General Court granted income from a public conveyance (the Charlestown ferry) to Harvard College and paid its president directly from the public treasury, higher education in America has been a hybrid of private and public; and over the centuries the distinction between the two has grown increasingly blurry.[15]

In early America, public subsidy of private institutions amounted to a sort of matching challenge, since individuals were expected to follow the lead of the magistrates and make donations of their own. This public-private partnership persists today in the form of tax exemption for private colleges and tax deductibility for their donors, as well as in the form of direct government grants that carry compliance conditions pertaining to hiring procedures, laboratory safety, and the like. As for public universities, they have gone deep into the business of raising private endowments, while private for-profit institutions are zealously exploiting the availability of public funds for low-income students, thereby joining the partnership as well.[16]

From time to time, the federal government has delivered shocks to this mixed system in the form of appropriations, regulations, or changes in the tax code. In the mid-nineteenth century, the Morrill Act created the land-grant institutions. In the mid-twentieth century, the GI Bill opened college to previously excluded groups. After World War II, a major science initiative, led by presidential advisor Vannevar Bush, created the now-familiar system of basic research through competitive funding awarded to universities by such government agencies as the National Science Foundation and the National Institutes of Health. In 1980, the Bayh-Dole Act opened up moneymaking prospects for both faculty and (mainly) research universities, and in 1986, Congress acted to end mandatory retirement, passing a law that made faculties older and probably made entry-level teaching positions scarcer—though colleges and universities were granted an exemption till 1994.

A few years ago, under President George W. Bush, another intervention from Washington seemed in the making. Convened by Secretary of Education Margaret Spellings, a federal commission took note of rising costs, low graduation rates, and the weakness of many college graduates in basic verbal and numerical skills. In response, some colleges, especially the more vulnerable ones, evinced a new urgency to make serious attempts at self-assessment before government stepped in, while the Ivies and other well-endowed institutions responded mainly by increasing subsidies to their relatively wealthy students. With less wealthy colleges and students in mind, some commentators now argue that in order to spare students and families from crippling debt, the standard duration of study for a bachelor's degree should be reduced from four years to three.[17] In fact, however, with the contraction of the job market, the opposite has been happening: the MA degree (master's programs in everything from statistics to museum studies have been burgeoning) is becoming a de facto fifth college year—but only, of course, for those who can afford to pay another year's tuition for another credential. It's another instance of the more needy getting less while the less needy get more.

Meanwhile, a privately developed test called the Collegiate Learning Assessment (CLA), designed to measure student progress from the first to the fourth year, has been adopted by a growing number of colleges, and many now participate in the National Survey of Student Engagement (NSSE), which seeks to measure how actively involved students are in their own education. A consortium of colleges, foundations, and lobbying groups has formed an organization called the New Leadership Alliance for Student Learning and Accountability, which has proposed a certificate, modeled on the Leadership in Energy and Environmental Design program (LEED), to be awarded to colleges that raise academic standards. And boards of trustees, which have mostly confined themselves to fiduciary oversight since the academic-freedom struggles of the early twentieth century, are beginning to take a more active role in monitoring the educational performance of the institutions they govern.[18] So far, it's too early to tell what good or harm will come of all this.

What's clear is that keeping the college idea alive for more than the privileged few is a huge challenge. With costs relentlessly rising, pressure is increasing on the idea of college as a capacious community with socioeconomic and ethnic diversity as well as

intellectual range. ~~Colleges in the same city or region are increas-~~
ingly tempted to consolidate academic departments—so that, say,
certain languages will be taught on one campus and others on
another. Some subjects and disciplines may be eliminated altogether, or provided through online instruction shared by multiple
institutions. Such cost-cutting strategies are, of course, likely to
take hold in less wealthy and prestigious institutions first, since
one component of prestige is the breadth of the course offerings.

In the meantime there are things, in theory at least, that government could do to help students from less affluent families get
into, and stay in, college. As Christopher Jencks has said with
admirable succinctness, "Making college a lot more affordable is
a challenge governments know how to meet, while making students learn a lot more is a challenge we do not currently know how
to meet. Under those circumstances, starting with affordability is
probably the best bet."[19] This would require making additional
expenditures for existing programs that serve low-income students, such as Pell grants and Perkins loans, and crediting some
portion of college tuition as a tax deduction. The economist
Ronald Ehrenberg has suggested that private and public colleges
should be rewarded with federal and state funds for each Pell
grant recipient who is graduated from their institution. Donald
Heller has made the more sweeping suggestion that all grants for
college students—institutional as well as governmental—should
be awarded on the basis of a needs analysis similar to that which
currently governs Pell grant expenditures.[20] The obvious problem with such proposals, sensible as they are, is that, unless they
are funded by shifting support from middle-class to needier students, they would require large new investments—two options
that seem politically impossible in the current context of anxiety
about government deficits.

Still, public discussion about higher education continues to focus on issues of cost and access, including the always-glamorous question of who gets to go to the most prestigious colleges. One problem with this focus is that getting in is by no means good enough. A great many low-income students who manage to start college never finish. A common response to this situation is to say that the real problem is our K–12 schools, and that, in fact, too many students go on to college rather than too few—but I have known only one parent who includes a child of his own in this assessment, which always seems to apply to other people's children.[21] Primary and secondary education doubtless need reform, and need it badly. But it would be folly for our colleges to wait. As one college president put it a century and a half ago, "whatever elementary instruction the schools fail to give, the college must supply."[22]

Not only should colleges do better at providing remedial help to students who need it, but they should recognize that their obligations begin with prospective students. More partnerships are needed between four-year colleges and community colleges, as well as collaborations linking colleges with local high schools and community organizations that work with high school students who are hoping, against the odds, to attend college.[23] Low-income families also need help in understanding the rationale for paying for education with future dollars—something that can be frightening to those who associate all forms of debt with exploitative lenders and the specter of default.[24] As for improving graduation rates, one striking finding from a recent study of public institutions is that children from low-income families are more likely to graduate if provided with "settings . . . that encourage close contact among students and between students and faculty members."[25] In short, what I have described in this book as the college idea still has the power to motivate young adults more than any other form of education we know.

3

So the problems are big, but despite recent demands that academia reform itself down to its foundations, big solutions—whether initiated from within or from without—are unlikely. Such demands are numerous and, often, shrill. One example is a recent book entitled *Crisis on Campus: A Bold Plan for Reforming Our Colleges and Universities*, based on an apocalyptic op-ed piece entitled "End the University as We Know It," that calls for the abolition of (among other things) tenure, academic departments, and the scholarly dissertation as a worse-than-worthless exercise in pedantry.[26] The premise here is that colleges and universities have become hopelessly sclerotic and removed from the real world. It's an old complaint. Emerson remarked a long time ago that "we are shut up in . . . college recitation rooms . . . & come out at last with a bellyful of words & do not know a thing. . . . We do not know an edible root in the woods. We cannot tell our course by the stars nor the hour of the day by the sun."[27]

Perhaps we really are more lost than ever. It is certainly true, as one former college president puts it, that most academic institutions are "organized anarchies," in which faculty "wander in and out of the decision-making process depending on circumstance and inclination."[28] Yet it is also true that much can be achieved—more than by crying crisis—when faculty and administrators work in a collaborative spirit on behalf of their students. There are plenty of examples of replicable "best practices" that have not been sufficiently replicated. One striking instance is the University of Maryland at Baltimore, where, under the leadership of President Freeman Hrabowski, graduation rates have markedly improved through a combination of mentoring, encouragement of structured group study, and apprenticeships to research faculty—with particularly impressive progress among minority students majoring in "STEM" (Science, Technology, Engineering, and Mathematics) fields. At Carnegie Mellon University, the "open learning initiative" is drawing widespread attention for its free online courses in which students get frequent feedback on how they are doing, and presentations and exercises are continually revised in response to evidence of how much students are learning.[29]

Even people who are skeptical, as I am, about the digital revolution as a great advance for learning must recognize the potential of the Internet to reduce the gap between the haves and havenots. Already today, access to archives or out-of-print books is no longer restricted to students with a "stack pass" at some great university library, and the long trip to consult a periodical or a rare newspaper can now be made in an instant through JSTOR, LexisNexis, and the like. Some educators see a bright future for college as a hybrid form of in-person and distance learning whereby students anywhere can "attend" lectures by a world-renowned lecturer via the web, then follow up in a discussion group with peers led by a local faculty member. And some believe that "mental attendance" is bound to be higher when such a student signs on at a time of his or her choosing rather than dozing in the back of a darkened lecture hall—or, for that matter, staying in bed.[30]

An exuberant vision of the future has recently been offered by Duke professor Cathy Davidson, who believes that, for young people accustomed to rapid-fire switching from texting to surfing to blogging, etc., multitasking is not a cause or symptom of distraction but an "ideal mode" of learning. In this vision, the classroom becomes a fluid and porous place—indeed hardly a place at all—in which authority for grading, and even for defining the subject of study, is shared by teacher and students, on the "crowd-sourcing" model of such collaborative entities as *Wikipedia*.[31] In some respects, this version of the college of the future is a vindication of the college of the past—a place in which students learn from their peers. What Davidson calls "collaboration by difference" is, in fact, the old idea of lateral learning under a new name: the idea that multiple perspectives contributed by students with different gifts and interests are not only desirable but essential. Her dynamic, improvisational college-to-come stands in bright contrast to the dark refrain one hears from many commentators who see higher education in decline. But in the end, utopian prophecies seem no more convincing than prophecies of doom.

While we await the high-tech college of the future, whatever it will turn out to be, it would be good to pay attention to cases where recalcitrant problems are yielding to low-tech solutions in the present. I suspect that multiyear contracts with (transparent, one hopes) review procedures will gradually overtake both lifetime tenure and casual hiring as the academic norm; but in the meantime, stability without sclerosis is the best condition for any college faculty. Denison University for one, has found that by carefully calibrating sabbatical schedules, it can shift from hiring temporary adjuncts to adding tenure-track professors even in small departments, so that students may count on faculty advisors who don't come and go from year to year. Beginning in 2010, Valparaiso University has been holding half-day workshops twice each academic year under the rubric "How the University Works," at which faculty meet with administrators in every sector of university governance from admissions to finance. The idea is to dispel the mystery and reduce the misunderstanding that can undermine trust between faculty and administrators, and to encourage informed debate of policy and practice. Good ideas are also emanating from study groups that span a range of institutions. The California Commission on General Education for the Twenty-first Century has proposed that at every research university, "one person, commanding a staff and a budget, should be in the cabinet of the president or chancellor with his or her primary responsibility to undergraduate education, with special attention to features of undergraduate education that transcend the interests of the departments."[32] It's a good proposal, since undergraduates rarely have a strong advocate in the president's inner circle.

Small changes, too, in classroom practice have been shown to yield large results—not only for students in the particular class, but, now that websites and blogs and social networks make it easy to get the word out, for students in other classes and colleges as well. Harvard physics professor Eric Mazur, having discovered that his students were doing more memorizing than thinking, shifted from the hour-long lecture to shorter periods of exposition alternated with ten-minute periods during which student breakout groups work collaboratively on an assigned problem. Students then report their results through an electronic feedback system, which tells the professor how well they have grasped the point he has just explained. If a significant number haven't understood it, he returns to it for further discussion before moving on. It's a way of restoring a dialogic dimension, even in a large class, to the monologic lecture.[33]

4

None of these innovations is, as the phrase goes, rocket science. They are commonsense responses to the plain fact that undergraduates easily get lost—which often starts with getting bored—

especially in institutions devoted to research and specialized instruction. All these experiments have in common something simple: they come from faculty who care. If good things are to happen to students, faculty must care, not only because this is the basic precondition of good teaching, but because, with a few minor exceptions such as teaching awards or, occasionally, supplementary pay for teaching certain required courses, the proffered rewards of academic life—promotions, raises, leaves—have nothing to do with demonstrated concern for students. In many academic institutions, teaching is its own reward.

Therefore, one obvious thing to do is to try to produce more teachers who care about teaching. This elementary but essential point has been made in one way or another by many recent critics of academia—Anthony Kronman, Louis Menand, Andrew Hacker, and Claudia Dreifus, to cite just a few. For all of them, the bogeyman is research—in the sense of narrowly focused inquiry into matters of marginal interest to young people in need of a general education.[34] I am obviously sympathetic to this view, which takes seriously the fact that the talents of the research scholar or scientist are not necessarily those of the teacher. If the same person gives evidence of both, it's a fortuitous convergence. Nearly a century ago, Max Weber noted that "one can be a preeminent scholar and at the same time an abominably poor teacher," and if we go back further still, we find Emerson making the mischievous suggestion that "a college professor should be elected by setting all the candidates loose on a miscellaneous gang of young men taken at large from the street. He who could get the ear of these youths after a certain number of hours . . . should be the professor."[35]

What all these critics have in common is the awareness that a gift for teaching cannot be certified by any advanced degree, and that zeal for teaching can be drained away by the professional training that allows one to become a college teacher in the first place. It doesn't have to be that way. No one should want America's universities to surrender their commitment to training researchers of the highest imagination and ambition, whether or not these people are well suited to teaching. The problem is not that universities are centers of research, but rather it's the way they use college teaching to subsidize the training of researchers. Our universities admit graduate students on the basis of scholarly promise, then assign them, in exchange for stipendiary support, and often with minimal preparation, to teach undergraduate discussion classes in, say, English or history, or sections of introductory science or math courses. "My graduate work," recalls Carol Geary Schneider, who holds a PhD in history and is now president of the Association of American Colleges and Universities, "had not included even an hour's worth of time on the real-world students I might find in my classroom, much less on the mysterious subject of 'learning.'"[36] Few graduate programs make much effort to distinguish between those who are qualified to do research in the library or lab and those who show promise for the classroom—and fewer make any systematic effort (this would be even better) to mitigate the distinction by helping good scholars and scientists become good teachers. Most applicants to a PhD program are never formally interviewed by teaching faculty, and once they arrive in graduate school, they are encouraged to think of teaching as an onerous obligation rather than an opportunity.

That this situation is taken for granted has been inadvertently confirmed by an exhaustively researched study whose results were recently published under the title *Educating Scholars: Doctoral Education in the Humanities* (2010). It's a densely statistical book showing rates of attrition, years-to-degree, patterns of postdoctoral employment, and so on; but it includes only a single brief mention of what the authors call "relevant preparation for later teaching careers." The mention comes in the context of a discussion of whether or not graduate teaching assistantships retard progress toward the degree. Similarly, the National Research Council bases its closely watched ranking of doctoral programs on criteria that have nothing to do with what doctoral programs do—or don't do—to prepare their graduates for college teaching.[37] These failures to consider teaching as an integral part of graduate education strike me as astonishing, but in most academic circles they don't seem to raise an eyebrow.

What we have here is a situation analogous to what it would mean if medical schools were to grant the MD degree to students who had never completed any clinical rotations. This might conceivably make sense for those determined to become "bench scientists" or to go into certain technical fields such as radiology, although even in such cases, a little human contact with patients wouldn't hurt—and sometimes a young person with expectations to the contrary discovers that working with patients is surprisingly satisfying. But the notion of sending a young physician to a patient's bedside without serious apprenticeship and mentoring is—as it should be—out of the question.

Moreover, unlike in graduate schools of arts and sciences, no candidate is admitted to an American medical school without a personal interview in which his or her fitness for the profession is (no doubt, imperfectly) assessed. In strictly financial terms, those who go into specialties or certain research fields are more amply rewarded than those who become primary care or family physicians—roughly analogous to becoming college teachers. But, without damage to the training of the former, medical schools have increasingly recognized the dignity and importance of the latter. By introducing opportunities for students to work in underserved communities, they have made progress toward closing the "schism between medicine as science and medicine as service." Many physicians now speak of "patient-centered" medicine as a main goal of the profession.[38] If we in academia are to break what Robert Maynard Hutchins long ago called "the vicious circle . . . in which the products of a bad system grow up to be the operators and perpetuators of it," it is high time that PhD programs take seriously their obligation to provide "student-centered" doctoral education—in the sense of preparing scholars to be teachers too.[39]

It shouldn't be all that hard. The distinction—or conflict—between research and teaching tends to be overstated, as one British writer nicely pointed out some years ago in response to a survey that asked faculty how they allotted their time between the two. That question, he said, is like asking a sheep "how much of its time is devoted to growing wool and how much to turning itself into mutton."[40] There is not—or at least ought not to be—a clear dividing line, and if it's a cliché to say, "my teaching enhances my scholarship" or "my scholarship makes me a better teacher," that's because both statements are often true. Passion for learning lies at the heart of scholarly and scientific investigation, and great practitioners have what one scientist called "radium of the soul" by which their students are inspired to push further, to revise or reject or extend the mentor's work. In a wonderful essay entitled "Research Strategy: Teach," the Cornell chemist Roald Hoffmann describes his creative process of discovery as inseparable from the act of explanation—explaining not only to himself but to multiple audiences, including undergraduates as well as professional peers. "The more I taught beginning classes, the more important it became to me to explain," he writes, and the more he realized that "the gleam of truth, or of a connection" is most likely to strike the mind "not in isolation, but in discourse with another person."[41] At their best, in other words, research is a form of teaching, and teaching is a form of research.

Yet future professors are seldom asked in graduate school to articulate the "why" of what they do, to learn to convey its significance to a lay audience, even to express for themselves the fascination they feel for it. In my own field of literary studies, for example, it would make eminent sense to include on every doctoral oral examination an opportunity for the candidate to make a case for why a given author might interest a college student. What makes him or her alive in the present moment? Why should this novel or poem or play written a hundred years ago still matter? In other words, how would you teach this subject? These questions may seem theoretically unsophisticated, but in fact they are hard questions—and, sooner or later, if one wants to be an effective teacher, they have to be confronted. If future teachers are not pressed to ask them from the start of their graduate training, the likelihood of their evading them—for now or forever—grows.[42]

The fact is that college teaching is a delicate and difficult art. It requires both confidence and tact. It means putting students under pressure, but it can degenerate into badgering or bullying. It requires making clear explanations of complex ideas. But sometimes it requires waiting out the silence after posing a difficult question—or, as Donald Finkel, a renowned teacher at Evergreen State College, once put it, "teaching with your mouth shut."[43] In training future scholars, we give far too little thought to these challenges, which, as teachers, all of them will face.

5

I have tried in this book to tell a story with a beginning, a middle (in relation to where we are today), but no end. It cannot be allowed to have an end. The American college faces a great many serious challenges—from the fiscal to the ethical and even, it might be said, the existential—but it is too precious an institution to be permitted to give up on its own ideals.

It began, as I have tried to show, in a spirit poised between hubris and humility. My view of the continuing pertinence of its religious origins may seem at odds with the intolerance of the clerics who founded it. They had no use for rival forms of Christianity, not to mention "heathens" such as Muslims and Jews, or the polytheistic "savages" amidst whom they found themselves living—except as candidates for conversion. They had their own kinds of blindness, self-deception, and cruelty. Yet when they were true to their convictions (are we sure that we are more so?), they tried to honor their cardinal belief that God in his omnipotence, not man in his presumption, determines the fate of every human being, and therefore that no outward mark—wealth or poverty, high or low social position, credentials or lack thereof—tells anything about the inward condition of the soul.

Even in our secular world, anyone concerned with America's colleges must still come to terms with the implications of these principles—including the linked truths that education is a mysterious process and that we should be slow to assume that any student is beyond its saving power. Perhaps the most daunting challenge facing those of us who believe in the universal value of liberal education is the challenge of conveying its value to anyone—policymakers, public officials, and even many academics—who has not personally experienced it. In this respect, too, we would do well to recall the Puritan view that the transformative power of a true education is "such a mystery as none can read but they that know it."[44]

If an old, and in many respects outmoded, religion seems an improbable touchstone for thinking about education today, perhaps a more plausible one is democracy. Surely it is an offense against democracy to presume that education should be reserved for the wellborn and the well-off. As Emerson put it in his great Phi Beta Kappa oration in 1837, "colleges can only highly serve us when . . . they gather from far every ray of various genius to their hospitable halls, and by the concentrated fires, set the hearts of their youth on flame. . . . Forget this, and our American colleges will recede in their public importance, whilst they grow richer every year."[45] He did not mean the word "genius" in our sense of extraordinary talent, but in the democratic sense that each individual possesses an irreplicable spirit. He meant that colleges should reach far, wide, and deep for their students and allow them, by their convergence, to ignite in one another a sense of the possibilities of democratic community.

No doubt, students with good preparation obtained in good high schools bring huge advantages with them to college. And since affluent applicants are overwhelmingly likely to have the stronger credentials, it will always be difficult for selective colleges to reconcile their twin principles of equity and excellence when they admit their new class every year. Yet it is often students of lesser means for whom college means the most—not just in the measurable sense of improving their economic competitiveness, but in the intellectual and imaginative enlargement it makes possible.

My own life in academia has been a privileged and insular one, and, to some readers, my emphasis in this book on a few selective colleges will seem to vitiate the general pertinence of the story I have tried to tell. But having observed and participated in classes at a wide range of colleges with students at all levels of preparation and sophistication, it's been my experience that whether they are studying accounting or philosophy, hotel management or history, the vast majority of college students are capable of engaging the kinds of big questions—questions of truth, responsibility, justice, beauty, among others—that were once assumed to be at the center of college education.

A number of leading educators have lately put this premise to the test. I'd like to mention here just two examples, one from each coast. At Stanford, a professor of philosophy, Debra Satz, with a colleague in political science, Rob Reich, started a program called "Hope House," in which faculty, assisted by undergraduate volunteers, discuss classic philosophical and literary texts with female addicts and ex-convicts living in a residential treatment center. At Bard College, in upstate New York, faculty teach literature, mathematics, history, and philosophy to inmates at the Eastern New York Correctional Facility. In each case, a word that figures frequently in descriptions of the experience is the word "joy."

In the Bard program, at each year's commencement (the term may sound ironic, since many of the graduates have only a remote chance for parole), students speak, according to Bard president Leon Botstein, of "the liberation of the mind . . . and their joy in the close, intense reading of texts, the working out of problem sets in mathematics, and the struggle they encountered in learning to reconsider deeply held prejudices and facile notions based on ignorance." At Stanford, the students "experienced joy and self-confidence by participating in a democratic community of inquiry" into deep questions raised by writers ranging from Immanuel Kant to Adrienne Rich on such issues as civil disobedience or the defensibility of lying on behalf of others or oneself. To bring such questions alive for their regular Stanford undergraduates, Satz and Reich report that they strain for historical examples such as lying to the Gestapo for the sake of a fugitive Jew—while the women in the "Hope House" program feel no disconnection between life and text, speaking readily and eloquently "from the cauldron of their own experiences."[46]

It is easy to dismiss such programs as the work of do-gooders making conscience-salving gestures; but anyone who witnesses or participates in this kind of teaching is likely to be chastened and moved. It is a reminder, as Botstein puts it, of "the connection between ethics and learning," which can be harder to establish among students "for whom the privilege of moving seamlessly from high school into college is taken for granted." In general, I think, we are too quick to assume that students with lesser preparation are unfit for education in this enlarging sense.

Quickest to assume so are today's entrepreneurs of for-profit education, such as the former director of the University of Phoenix (now by far America's largest college, with five times as many students as the largest public university, Ohio State), who tells us that "I'm happy that there are places in the world where people sit down and think. We need that. But that's very expensive. And not everybody can do that. So for the vast majority of folks who don't get that privilege, then I think it's a business."[47] The putative realism of this point of view is a surrender of America's democratic promise. At my own university we have an undergraduate division that admits students who may have started years ago at another college, then gone to work, or to war, before resuming their studies. They are frequently admitted into the same courses with highly credentialed students of traditional college age, where, it turns out, those with the most searching minds are sometimes military veterans who have arrived in the classroom via some unheralded community college and a tour in the army on a battlefield in Afghanistan or Iraq.

Perhaps the brightest spot in the contemporary landscape of American higher education is the resurgence of interest in engaging students in civic life beyond campus. "Community service" organizations have long been a feature of most colleges, but explicit connection of coursework with service work is relatively new, and growing. In courses on such subjects as immigration, the environment, public health, and education, among others, students integrate their reading and writing assignments with volunteer work helping immigrant families cope with public bureaucracies, doing research for an environmental advocacy group, tutoring at-risk children, or assisting the elderly—sometimes through partnerships that formally link a college with a community organization. Much of the impetus for such work comes from the students themselves, who, despite everything I have said about the problems and pathologies of contemporary college culture, are often brimming with ideals and energy and hope, and have a craving for meaningful work.

There is also a growing movement promoting education for citizenship by engaging students on issues of constitutional interpretation provoked by debate over current issues such as gay marriage, gun control, or civil liberties in wartime. One organization called Project Pericles sponsors an annual national conference, "Debating for Democracy," in which students from some thirty participating colleges come together for public debate and receive critiques from leading public figures on the quality of their research and their arguments.[48]

Such initiatives are continuous with the best traditions of the American college as an institution devoted not only to personal advancement but to the public good. Some of our leading colleges are showing leadership in taking this tradition seriously—as in Amherst's commitment to providing students in nearby community colleges with mentoring support and, for strong students, an opportunity to transfer to Amherst itself; or Yale's engagement with the city of New Haven by forming partnerships with local schools and generally accepting its responsibility to mitigate the "town-gown" tension that elite institutions have often inflamed. On a recent visit to The University of Tulsa, I learned that the university provides up to eight hours per month of paid leave for staff who wish to devote that time to community service. Such actions bespeak a recognition that in any genuine community—an aspiration fundamental to the original conception of college—self-interest and public interest are not at odds, but are two names for the same thing.

The institution I have explored in this book is a very old one. Yet one of the pleasures of the teaching life is to witness its renewal with every incoming class. Much of what has been true of students will always be true. A hundred and forty years ago, the president of Yale wrote of "the leisure and curiosity of this morning of life," and of "the zest with which its novel experiences ... are enjoyed." In our own day a former president of Amherst writes of a young man experiencing in college the "stirring and shaping, perhaps for the first time in his life, [of] actual convictions—not just gut feelings—among his friends and, more important, further down, in his own soul."[49]

College should be much more than a place that winnows the "best" from the rest. It should be a transit point for those whom Lionel Trilling called "midway people," whose "movement from social group to social group ... makes for the uncertainty of their moral codes, their confusion, their indecision"—that is, for young Americans, who, more than their counterparts in other nations, have all and always been "midway people" in Trilling's sense.[50] A college should not be a haven from worldly contention, but a place where young people fight out among and within themselves contending ideas of the meaningful life, and where they discover that self-interest need not be at odds with concern for one another. We owe it to posterity to preserve and protect this institution. Democracy depends on it.

ACKNOWLEDGMENTS

After more than thirty years as a college teacher, I have accumulated so many debts to students, colleagues, and friends that I must confine myself here to acknowledging those who have had a direct effect on the writing of this book.

First, thanks are due to the Committee on Public Lectures at Princeton University for the invitation to deliver the Stafford Little Lectures, of which this book is an expansion and elaboration. I am grateful to Peter Dougherty, Hanne Winarsky, and Kathleen Cioffi at Princeton University Press, who waited patiently while I developed the lectures into a book, as well as to the two readers who made invaluable suggestions in response to the manuscript. Joan Gieseke improved the book with her careful copyediting, as did Julie Shawvan, who created the thorough index.

The largest influences on my own classroom practice have been the memorable teachers I encountered as a student, and those from whom I have learned since. I think especially of Phil Schwartz, whom I assisted in an Upward Bound program when I was still in high school; of Sara Bershtel, who, when I was in college, showed me how exciting a place a classroom could be; and of the late James Shenton, whose televised lectures on American history enthralled me long ago, and who, years later, welcomed me as a colleague. The enduring example of my mentor, the late Alan Heimert, is in my mind every time I give a lecture, lead a discussion, or meet with a student. I've had the privilege of teaching a college seminar with Steven Marcus, who set a daunting standard, and, more recently, an undergraduate course on equity and access in higher education, with Roger Lehecka, whose devotion to students and knowledge of the subject are without parallel in my experience, and who provided incisive readings of the manuscript at several stages of revision. The students in that course have been inspiring in their passionate commitment to educational equity as well as excellence.

I owe a great deal to the late Barbara Epstein, and to Robert Silvers, for inviting me to try out my thoughts in several essay-reviews for the *New York Review of Books*, parts of which appear in this book in different form. Many years ago, when I had just started thinking about a subject for an earlier book, Barbara asked me a question—"How will you make it a story?"—that continues to challenge me whenever I set out to write anything. As everyone knows who has worked with Bob, writing for him is an education in itself.

I am also grateful to Paul Baumann at *Commonweal*, Lewis Lapham at *Lapham's Quarterly*, and Alex Star at the *New York Times Magazine*, who commissioned reviews and essays that helped my thinking and have been partially incorporated in this book.

Some of the ideas and formulations in the foregoing pages were tried out before audiences who engaged me in spirited discussion and debate. I think particularly of the members of a seminar organized by Ellen Lagemann and supported by Sue Anne Weinberg, and of the graduate students who enrolled in a colloquium on higher education that I have offered regularly over the past decade at Columbia, initially in collaboration with my colleague Casey Blake. For supporting that colloquium, thanks are due to the Andrew W. Mellon Foundation, where Joseph Meisel, now Deputy Provost of Brown University, was especially helpful. I am grateful, too, to the Spencer Foundation for a grant that allowed me an uninterrupted summer of reading and writing.

For invitations to speak to, and with, educators concerned with the needs of college students, I wish to thank President John DeGioia and Provost James O'Donnell at Georgetown University; Provost Mark Schwehn and Assistant Provost David Owens at Valparaiso University; President David Levinson and Professor Steven Berizzi at Norwalk Community College; President Nathan Hatch of Wake Forest University; Professor Carl Eby and colleagues at the University of South Carolina at Beaufort; Aine Donovan and her colleagues at the Center for Ethics at Dartmouth College, especially James Murphy of the Daniel Webster Program, who made helpful suggestions in response to my talk; Dave Guthrie at Geneva College; Simon Head and Jane Tylus at New York University; Debra Satz, Dean of Humanities at Stanford; Pat McPherson and Judith Shapiro at the American Philosophical Society; Richard Ekman of the Council of Independent Colleges; Jerry Lucido of the Center for Enrollment Research, Policy, and Practice at the University of Southern California; Lloyd Thacker of the Education Conservancy; Denise Dutton at The University of Tulsa; Thomas Hibbs at Baylor University; Craig Warren and his colleagues in the College English Association; Kathleen Little at the College Board; Charles Eisendrath and the 2010–2011 Knight-Wallace Fellows at the University of Michigan; Ted Bracken of the Consortium on Financing Higher Education; Carolyn De La Pena at the University of California, Davis; Joseph Luzzi at Bard College; Linda Halpern, past president of the American Council of Academic Deans; Dean John Harrington at Fordham University; Richard Morrill and Donna Heiland of the Teagle Foundation, for their thoughtful readings of the manuscript; and W. Robert Connor, former president of the Teagle Foundation, who invited me to participate in several "listenings" on the future of higher education. All the gatherings listed above included educators of high integrity who helped me to sharpen my thinking and to take my thoughts in new directions.

My thanks go as well to the creators of *Avenue Q*, Robert Lopez and Jeff Marx, and their publisher, Alfred Music Publishing, for permission to quote the lyrics to "I Wish I Could Go to College." Copyright © 2003 Only for Now, Inc. and Fantasies Come True, Inc. All rights on Behalf of Only for Now, Inc. administered by Warner-Tamerlane Publishing Corp. All rights reserved. Used by permission. Philip Larkin's poem, "Talking in Bed," from *Collected Poems* by Philip Larkin is reprinted by permission of Farrar, Straus and Giroux, LLC, Faber and Faber, Ltd., and the Society of Authors, Literary Representative of the Estate of Philip Larkin. Copyright © 1988, 2003 by the Estate of Philip Larkin.

In my own college years, many good things happened to me. By far the best was meeting my wife, Dawn. Over the years since, her devotion to her students—undergraduates as well as the graduate students whom she has mentored as they strive to become teachers themselves—has been a chastening example. She continues to be my most demanding reader, but that is only one among countless reasons why she has my gratitude beyond measure.

NOTES

Introduction

1. Malcolm Gladwell, "The Order of Things: What College Rankings Really Tell Us," *New Yorker*, February 14 and 21, 2011, p. 72.

2. Clark Kerr, *The Uses of the University*, 5th ed. (1963; Cambridge: Harvard University Press, 2001), p. 49.

3. Jaimes Amber, "Neouniversitas," *Harvard Crimson*, October 12, 2010.

4. Abigail Adams to John Adams, August 14, 1776, in *The Book of Abigail and John: Selected Letters of the Adams Family, 1762–1784*, ed. L. H. Butterfield, Marc Friedlaender, and Mary-Jo Kline (Cambridge: Harvard University Press, 1975), p. 152; David Starr Jordan, quoted in Julie A. Reuben, *The Making of the Modern University: Intellectual Transformation and the Marginalization of Morality* (Chicago: University of Chicago Press, 1996), p. 253.

5. Scott McNealy, chairman of Sun Microsystems, quoted in Anan Giridharadas, "Virtual Classrooms Could Create a Marketplace of Knowledge," *New York Times*, November 6, 2009.

6. Bowen, commencement address at the graduate school of Indiana University, May 6, 2011. Alison Wolf, *Does Education Matter? Myths about Education and Economic Growth* (London: Penguin Books, 2002), p. 247.

7. Earnest Earnest, quoted in Jerome Karabel, *The Chosen* (Boston: Houghton-Mifflin, 2005), p. 19.

8. Anya Kamenetz, *DIYU: Edupunks, Edupreneurs, and the Coming Transformation of Higher Education* (White River Junction, VT: Chelsea Green, 2010), p. 34.

9. For a detailed analysis of the growing gap between well-funded and poorly funded colleges, see the report *Trends in College Spending: 1999–2009* (September 2011), by the Delta Cost Project and the Lumina Foundation, http://www.deltacostproject .org/resources/pdf/Trends2011_Final_090711.pdf.

Chapter One. What Is College For?

1. This experience pertains mainly to colleges where most students are of "traditional" age. The number of "nontraditional" students, i.e., those who have come to college at a later stage of life, has been rapidly growing.

2. Shulman, quoted in Donald N. Levine, *Powers of the Mind: The Reinvention of Liberal Learning in America* (Chicago: University of Chicago Press, 2006), p. 130.

3. Recent studies of student evaluations have found that students tend to give good reviews "to instructors who are easy graders or who are good looking," and lesser reviews to women and instructors born outside the United States. The largest such study, at Ohio State University, finds "no correlation between professor evaluations and the learning that is actually taking place." See *InsideHigherEd.com*, January 29, 2007.

4. *New England's First Fruits* (1643), in Samuel Eliot Morison, *The Founding of Harvard College* (Cambridge: Harvard University Press, 1935), p. 432.

5. Wallace Stegner, *Crossing to Safety* (New York: Penguin Books, 1988), p. 31.

6. Michael S. McPherson and Morton Owen Schapiro, "The Future Economic Challenges for the Liberal Arts Colleges," in *Distinctively American: The Residential Liberal Arts Colleges*, ed. Steven Koblik and Stephen R. Graubard (New Brunswick, NJ: Transaction, 2000), p. 50.

7. For a statistical portrait of undergraduate education, see the annual "Almanac of Higher Education," published most recently by the *Chronicle of Higher Education*, August 26, 2011.

8. Mark Lilla's lecture, "The Soldier, The Sage, The Saint, and the Citizen" (delivered on April 23, 2010), is posted on the Columbia University website: http://www.college.columbia.edu/core/lectures/spring2010-0.

9. See Suniya S. Luthar and Shawn J. Latendresse, "Children of the Affluent: Challenges to Well-Being," *Current Directions in Psychological Science* 14, no. 1 (February 2005): 49–53.

10. As early as 1869, Charles W. Eliot, Harvard's first president without a clerical background, dismissed "the notion that education consists in the authoritative inculcation of what the teacher deems true," and declared "the very word 'education'" to be "a standing protest against dogmatic teaching" (Eliot, inaugural address as president of Harvard [1869], in *American Higher Education: A Documentary History*, 2 vols., ed. Richard Hofstadter and Wilson Smith [Chicago: University of Chicago Press, 1961], 2:606). There are, alas, still dogmatic teachers, although their numbers are exaggerated and their dogma is more likely today to be political than theological.

11. Laurence R. Veysey, *The Emergence of the American University* (Chicago: University of Chicago Press, 1965), p. 271.

12. Charles Franklin Thwing, *The American College: What It Is and What It May Become* (New York: Platt and Peck, 1914), p. 97. I am grateful to Steven Wheatley of the American Council of Learned Societies for drawing my attention to this book. The English professor was Fred Lewis Pattee, quoted in Gerald Graff, *Professing Literature: An Institutional History* (Chicago: University of Chicago Press, 1987), p. 107.

13. Trilling, "The Uncertain Future of the Humanistic Educational Ideal" (1974), in *The Last Decade: Essays and Reviews, 1965–75* (New York: Harcourt, Brace, Jovanovich, 1979), pp. 160–76.

14. Sam Lipsyte, *The Ask* (New York: Farrar, Straus, and Giroux, 2010), p. 51.

15. *Spencer Foreman, MD in First Person: An Oral History* (Chicago: American Hospital Association Center for Hospital Administration

and Health Care Administration History and Health Research and Educational Trust, 2008), p. 6.

16. Burton J. Bledstein, *The Culture of Professionalism: The Middle Class and the Development of Higher Education in America* (New York: W. W. Norton, 1978), p. 227; Veysey, *Emergence of the University*, p. 269.

17. Morison, *Founding of Harvard*, p. 229.

18. Roth, *Indignation* (New York: Vintage Books, 2009), p. 49. "Tufts U. Bans Student Sex When Roommates Are Present," *Chronicle of Higher Education*, September 28, 2009. For an account of social life on the same campus, see "Lady Power," by Nancy Bauer, chair of the Philosophy Department at Tufts: "Visit an American college campus on a Monday morning and you'll find any number of amazingly ambitious and talented young women wielding their brain power, determined not to let anything—including a relationship with some needy, dependent man—get in their way. Come back on a party night, and you'll find many of these same girls (they stopped calling themselves 'women' years ago) wielding their sexual power, dressed as provocatively as they dare, matching the guys drink for drink—and then hook-up for hook-up. . . . When they're on their knees in front of a worked-up guy they just met at a party, they genuinely do feel powerful—sadistic, even. After all, though they don't stand up and walk away, they in principle could. But the morning after, students routinely tell me, they are vulnerable to what I've come to call the 'hook-up hangover.' They'll see the guy in the quad and cringe. Or they'll find themselves wishing in vain for more—if not for a prince (or a vampire, maybe) to sweep them off their feet, at least for the guy actually to have programmed their number into his cell phone the night before. When the text doesn't come, it's off to the next party." Opinionator.blogs.nytimes.com, June 20, 2010.

19. Thorstein Veblen, *The Higher Learning in America* (1918: repr. New York: Hill and Wang, 1957), pp. 101, 99.

20. Romano, "Will the Book Survive Generation Text?" *Chronicle of Higher Education*, August 29, 2010; Kevin Kiley, "Long Reads," *InsideHigherEd.com*, May 12, 2011; Clydesdale, "Wake up and Smell the New Epistemology," *Chronicle of Higher Education*, January, 23,

2009; Menand, *The Marketplace of Ideas: Reform and Resistance in the American University* (New York: W. W. Norton, 2010), p. 19.

21. Bowen, preface to *Jefferson and Education*, ed. Jennings L. Wagoner Jr. (Chapel Hill: University of North Carolina Press, 2004), pp. 11–12.

22. Richard Vedder, *Going Broke by Degree: Why College Costs Too Much* (Washington DC: American Enterprise Institute, 2004), p. 52; Brody, quoted in Dale Keiger, "Measuring the Unmeasurable," *Johns Hopkins Magazine*, November, 2008, p. 29.

23. The incidence of cheating is hard to measure, but one authority on the subject, Donald McCabe of Rutgers University, finds that the number of students reporting "cut and paste" plagiarism using Internet sources quadrupled between 1999 and 2001. McCabe also describes a sharp rise over the last four decades in the number of students reporting "unpermitted collaboration" (academicintegrity.org/cai_research.asp). Drawing on McCabe's research, David Callahan, *The Cheating Culture: Why More Americans Are Doing Wrong to Get Ahead* (New York: Harcourt, 2004), p. 217, estimates that serious cheating in college increased by 30 to 35 percent during the 1990s. As for drinking, many studies confirm the high incidence of binge drinking and substance abuse among college students. See, for example, "Wasting the Best and the Brightest: Substance Abuse at America's Colleges and Universities," report from the National Center on Addiction and Substance Abuse at Columbia University, March, 2007, available at http://www.casacolumbia.org/templates/Publications_Reports.aspx#r111, which estimates that roughly half of all full-time college students binge drink or abuse drugs at least once a month.

24. Harriet Beecher Stowe, *My Wife and I* (New York, 1871), pp. 76–77.

25. Harry Lewis, *Excellence without a Soul: How a Great University Forgot Education* (New York: Public Affairs, 2006), p. 17. The phrase "service-station conception" comes from Robert Maynard Hutchins, *The Higher Learning in America* (New Haven, CT: Yale University Press, 1936), p. 6.

26. Riley, quoted in Mildred Garcia, "A New Model of Liberal Learning for the 21st Century," *DailyBreeze.com*, November 23, 2009. Garcia, a

staunch defender of liberal education, is president of California State University at Dominguez Hills, a community college serving a large minority population. President Obama, quoted in *Politico*, February 24, 2009.

27. Alison Wolf, *Does Education Matter? Myths about Education and Economic Growth* (London: Penguin, 2002), p. 18: "The more educated you are, the more likely you are to be in work, to stay in work, and to enjoy stable, long-term employment on a permanent contract." There is also evidence that an associate's degree from a two-year college, or completing even a year or two at a four-year college, has measurable economic value. Relative to their starting point, students who gain the most in economic terms seem to be those from poor families, or from families where no one has previously attended college, or from minority groups with lower college-going rates. See David Glenn, "Disadvantaged Students May Benefit Most from Attending College," *Chronicle of Higher Education*, April 1, 2010. Recent data are available in "The College Payoff: Education, Occupation, Lifetime Earnings," http://cew .georgetown.edu/collegepayoff/, released on August 5, 2011, by the Georgetown University Center on Education and the Workforce, in partnership with the Lumina Foundation.

28. See Clifford Adelman, *The Spaces Between Numbers: Getting International Data on Higher Education Straight* (Washington DC: Institute for Higher Education Policy, 2009), and Jane V. Wellman, *Apples and Oranges in the Flat World: A Layperson's Guide to International Comparisons of Postsecondary Education* (Washington DC: American Council on Education, 2007).

29. Brian K. Fitzgerald, "Missed Opportunities: Has College Opportunity Fallen Victim to Policy Drift?" *Change* 36, no. 4 (July–August 2004): 14. The estimates of chances to attend college are cited, with permission, from a talk given on March 5, 2010, by Eugene Tobin, former president of Hamilton College, currently program officer on higher education at the Andrew W. Mellon Foundation. Tobin was drawing on Ross Douthat, "Does Meritocracy Work?" *Atlantic Monthly*, November 2005, p. 120; and William G. Bowen, Martin A. Kurzweil, and Eugene M. Tobin, *Equity and Excellence in Ameri-*

can Higher Education (Charlottesville: University of Virginia Press, 2005), pp. 77–94.

30. Danette Gerald and Kati Haycock, "Engines of Inequality: Diminishing Equity in the Nation's Premier Public Universities" (Washington DC: Education Trust, 2006).

31. See, for example, Charles Murray, "Are Too Many People Going to College?" *The American* (Journal of the American Enterprise Institute) 2, no. 5 (September–October 2008): 40–49.

32. Ann Larson, "Higher Education's Big Lie," *InsideHigherEd.com*, June 3, 2010; and Jacques Steinberg, "Plan B: Skip College," *New York Times*, May 14, 2010.

33. Jan J. Barendregt et al., "The Health Care Costs of Smoking," *New England Journal of Medicine* 337 (October 9, 1997): 1052–57.

34. In Lester J. Cappon, ed., *The Adams-Jefferson Letters: The Complete Correspondence between Thomas Jefferson and Abigail and John Adams* (New York: Simon and Schuster, 1971), p. 480.

35. Smith made this statement at Oxford in 1914.

36. In a talk delivered at the National Convention for Teachers of English, published in Neil Postman and Charles Weingartner, *Teaching as a Subversive Activity* (New York: Delacorte, 1969), Postman credited the phrase "crap detector" to Ernest Hemingway as a term describing the one thing necessary for good writing.

37. Anthony Kronman, *Education's End: Why Our Colleges and Universities Have Given Up on the Meaning of Life* (New Haven, CT: Yale University Press, 2007), pp. 172–73.

38. Victor E. Ferrall Jr., *Liberal Arts on the Brink* (Cambridge: Harvard University Press, 2011), p. 8.

39. Bruce Kimball, *Orators and Philosophers: A History of the Idea of Liberal Education* (1986), quoted in Francis Oakley, *Community of Learning: The American College and the Liberal Arts Tradition* (New York: Oxford University Press, 1992), p. 51.

40. Arnold, *Culture and Anarchy* (1869), ed. Samuel Lipman (New Haven, CT: Yale University Press, 1994), p. 5.

41. John Henry Newman, *The Idea of a University* (1852), ed. Frank M. Turner (New Haven, CT: Yale University Press, 1996), p. 81.

42. My impression is at odds with that of Richard Arum and Josipa Roksa, *Academically Adrift: Limited Learning on College Campuses* (Chicago: University of Chicago Press, 2011), who estimate that today's college students, on average, spend only twelve hours per week studying (p. 69). Arum and Roksa suggest that students at highly selective colleges spend somewhat more—around fifteen hours. Other studies, such as that of Philip Babcock and Mindy Marks, summarized in *Leisure College USA: The Decline in Student Study Time* (Washington DC: American Enterprise Institute, 2010), conclude that study time has declined by roughly 50 percent over the half century since 1961. For a more nuanced view, see Alexander C. McCormick, "It's About Time: What to Make of Reported Declines in How Much College Students Study," *Liberal Education* 97, no. 1 (Winter 2011): 30–39 (published by the Association of American Colleges and Universities). McCormick calls attention to such factors as "efficiency gains due to new technologies" (by which he means word processing versus the longhand writing or mechanical typewriting of fifty years ago), as well as to the different meanings of "week" that students have in mind (some mean five days, others seven) in responding to survey questions about their study habits.

43. Owen Johnson, *Stover at Yale* (1912; Boston: Little, Brown, 1926), p. 234.

Chapter Two. Origins

1. Aristotle, *Politics*, Book 7; H. I. Marrou, *A History of Education in Antiquity* (New York: New American Library, 1964), p. 402; Oakley, *Community of Learning*, p. 18.

2. Morison, *Founding of Harvard*, p. 37.

3. Thomas Wentworth Higginson, *The Life of Francis Higginson* (New York, 1891), pp. 11–12.

4. Morison, *Founding of Harvard*, pp. 80–81.

5. Frederick Rudolph, *The American College and University: A History* (1962) (Athens: University of Georgia Press, 1990), p. 90, suggests that early American colleges failed to replicate this plan because they could not afford the cost of such elaborate construction.

6. Morison, *Founding of Harvard*, p. 82.

7. Alan Heimert, "Let Us Now Praise Famous Men," *Cambridge Review* 106 (November 1985): 177–82.

8. Jennifer Tomase, "Tale of John Harvard's Surviving Book," *Harvard University Gazette*, November 1, 2007.

9. Lawrence Cremin, *American Education: The Colonial Experience* (New York: Simon and Schuster, 1979), pp. 214, 221.

10. Morison, *Founding of Harvard*, p. 249.

11. Jonathan Edwards, *Scientific and Philosophical Writings*, ed. Wallace E. Anderson (New Haven, CT: Yale University Press, 1980), p. 306.

12. Newman, *The Idea of a University*, ed. Turner, p. 76; Edwards, *Scientific and Philosophical Writings*, p. 344. Frederick Barnard, quoted in Reuben, *Making of the Modern University*, p. 22.

13. Horatio Greenough, *Form and Function: Remarks on Art, Design, and Architecture*, ed. Harold A. Small (Berkeley: University of California Press, 1947), p. 74. The essays constituting this volume were originally published in 1853.

14. Morison, *Founding of Harvard*, p. 252. Daniel Coit Gilman, quoted in Veysey, *Emergence of the University*, p. 161.

15. Lewis, quoted by Bowen in his commencement address at Indiana University, May 6, 2011.

16. Jerome Karabel, *The Chosen: The Hidden History of Admission and Exclusion at Harvard, Yale, and Princeton* (Boston: Houghton Mifflin, 2005), p. 51.

17. Quoted in James O. Freedman, *Liberal Education and the Public Interest* (Iowa City: University of Iowa Press, 2003), p. 107.

18. Newman, *Idea of a University*, ed. Turner, p. 83.

19. Oakley, *Community of Learning*, pp. 50–51.

20. Seneca, *Moral Epistles*, no. 88 ("On Liberal and Vocational Studies"), 3 vols., trans. Richard M. Gummere (Loeb Classical Library) (Cambridge: Harvard University Press, 1917–1925), 2:353–55.

21. Emerson, journal entry, April 20, 1834, in *Emerson in His Journals*, ed. Joel Porte (Cambridge: Harvard University Press, 1982), p. 123.

22. Ascham, quoted in Morison, *Founding of Harvard*, p. 61; Bledstein, *The Culture of Professionalism*, p. 243. This number may be somewhat

misleading, since the range of ages contributing to the average was relatively wide. See James Morgan Hart, in Hofstadter and Smith, *Higher Education: A Documentary History*, 2:579. "Normal age" is Charles W. Eliot's phrase, in Hofstadter and Smith, eds., *Higher Education*, 2:705.

23. Cotton, *Christ the Fountaine of Life*, p. 98; Emerson, journal entry, September 13, 1831, in Porte, ed., *Emerson in His Journals*, p. 80.

24. William G. Perry Jr., *Forms of Ethical and Intellectual Development in the College Years*, ed. L. Lee Knefelkamp (1970; San Francisco: Jossey-Bass, 1999), pp. xii, 3.

25. Cotton Mather, *Magnalia Christi Americana*, 2 vols. (1702; Hartford, CT, 1853), 1:273, 260.

26. Perry, *Forms of Development*, p. 37.

27. John Davenport, *The Saint's Anchor-Hold* (London, 1682), p. 132. The concept of stereotype threat was introduced in 1995 by Claude M. Steele and Joshua Aronson in their article "Stereotype Threat and the Intellectual Test Performance of African Americans," *Journal of Personality and Social Psychology* 69 (5): 797–811.

28. Weber, "Science as a Vocation" (1918) in *From Max Weber: Essays in Sociology*, ed. Hans Gerth and C. Wright Mills (New York: Oxford University Press, 1958), p. 136; Henry Adams, *The Education of Henry Adams* (1918; Boston: Houghton Mifflin, 1973), pp. 80–81.

29. William James, *Varieties of Religious Experience* (1902; New York: Collier Books, 1973), p. 172.

30. Nate Kornell and Janet Metcalfe, "'Blockers' Do Not Block Recall during Tip-of-the-Tongue States," *Metacognition and Learning* 1 (2006): 248–61.

31. Janet Metcalfe, "Improving Student Learning: Empirical Findings," PowerPoint presentation, Columbia University Center for Teaching and Learning, January 29, 2009. "A mind must work to grow" is from C. W. Eliot, in Hofstadter and Smith, eds., *Higher Education*, 2:610. "Passive absorption" is quoted from John Dewey, in Donald Levine, *Powers of the Mind*, p. 81.

32. John Cotton, *A Treatise of the Covenant of Grace* (London, 1671), p. 154.

33. Cotton Mather, *Magnalia Christi Americana* (1702), in Hofstadter and Smith, eds., *Higher Education*, 1:15.

34. Hawthorne, *The Scarlet Letter* (1850; New York: Penguin Books, 1986), p. 25; Newman, *Idea of a University*, ed. Turner, p. 77; Dewey, in *The Philosophy of John Dewey*, 2 vols., ed. John J. McDermott (New York: G. P. Putnam's Sons, 1973), 2:447; Perry, *Forms of Development*, ed. Knefelkamp, pp. xxxiii, 120. Writing in this tradition, Donald Levine, former dean of the college at the University of Chicago, defines a true college as "a kindred assemblage constituted by diversity of opinion" (*Powers of the Mind*, p. 67).

35. Jarrell, *Pictures from an Institution* (1952; Chicago: University of Chicago Press, 1986), p. 82.

36. John S. Coolidge, *The Pauline Renaissance in England* (Oxford: Oxford University Press, 1970), pp. 49–50; John Cotton, *Christ the Fountaine of Life* (London, 1651), p. 156.

37. Interview with Yongfang Chen and Li Wan, "A True Liberal Arts Education," *InsideHigherEd.com*, October 16, 2009.

38. DuBois, *Dusk of Dawn: An Essay Toward an Autobiography of a Race Concept* (1940; New York: Schocken, 1968), pp. 38, 33.

39. Cotton, *Christ the Fountaine of Life*, p. 200.

40. Robert Greene, quoted in Paul Seaver, *The Puritan Lectureships: The Politics of Religious Dissent, 1560–1662* (Stanford: Stanford University Press, 1970), p. 40.

41. Harry Stout, *The New England Soul: Preaching and Religious Culture in Colonial New England* (New York: Oxford University Press, 1986), p. 4.

42. Rogers, in *The Colleges and the Public, 1787–1862*, ed. Theodore Rawson Crane (New York: Teachers College Press, Columbia University, 1963), p. 47. For a searching treatment of Rogers's thought and career, see Philip Alexander, *A Widening Sphere: Evolving Cultures at MIT* (Cambridge, MA: MIT Press, 2011).

43. Santayana, *Character and Opinion in the United States* (1920; New York: W. W. Norton, 1967), p. 96.

44. Morison, *Founding of Harvard*, p. 85.

45. Franklin, "Proposals Relating to the Education of Youth in Pennsylvania" (1749) in *Benjamin Franklin: Representative Selections*, ed. Frank Luther Mott (New York: Hill and Wang, 1962), p. 206.

46. William G. Durden, "Reclaiming the Distinctiveness of American Higher Education," *Liberal Education* 93, no. 2 (Spring 2007): 40.

Chapter Three. From College to University

1. See James T. Axtell, "Dr. Wheelock's Little Red School," chap. 4 in *The European and the Indian: Essays in the Ethnohistory of Colonial America* (New York: Oxford University Press, 1981).

2. Thomas Jefferson Wertenbaker, *Princeton: 1746–1896* (Princeton, NJ: Princeton University Press, 1946), p. 18.

3. Jefferson to Adams, in Cappon, ed., *Adams-Jefferson Letters*, p. 599.

4. Charles A. Brixted, *Five Years in an English University*, 2 vols. (New York, 1852), 1:106. Thanks to James O'Donnell for alerting me to this book. For the growth of colleges in the 1820s, see David B. Potts, *Liberal Education for a Land of Colleges: Yale's Reports of 1828* (New York: Palgrave Macmillan, 2010), p. 9.

5. Richard Hofstadter, *Academic Freedom in the Age of the College* (1955; repr. New Brunswick, NJ: Transaction, 1996), pp. 223–24.

6. Kamenetz, *DIYU*, p. 10.

7. Charles Sumner, quoted in David Donald, *Charles Sumner and the Coming of the Civil War* (New York: Knopf, 1961), p. 14; Adams, *Education*, pp. 54–55.

8. Bledstein, *Culture of Professionalism*, p. 229. Diary of Hugh Gwynn, 1850–51; coll. 298, folder 30 (manuscript collections, Wilson Library of the University of North Carolina at Chapel Hill), p. 67.

9. Reuben, *Making of the Modern University* (1996), is a distinguished exception.

10. See Potts, *Liberal Education for a Land of Colleges*, pp. 16–19.

11. James McPherson, *The Abolitionist Legacy* (Princeton, NJ: Princeton University Press, 1975), p. 7.

12. Bowen et al., *Equity and Excellence*, p. 21.

13. Charles Dickens, *American Notes for General Circulation* (1842; London: Penguin Books, 1972), p. 77.

14. D. H. Meyer, *The Instructed Conscience: The Shaping of the American National Ethic* (Philadelphia: University of Pennsylvania Press, 1972), pp. 68, 66.

15. James McCosh, *The Divine Government, Physical and Moral* (New York, 1852), p. 320.

16. Noah Porter, *The American Colleges and the American Public* (1870), in *Education in the United States: A Documentary History*, 5 vols., ed. Sol Cohen (New York: Random House, 1974), 3:1474.

17. Carnegie, quoted in Frank Donoghue, *The Last Professors: The Corporate University and the Fate of the Humanities* (New York: Fordham University Press, 2008), p. 4.

18. Dunne, "Education of the Young," in *Mr. Dooley's Philosophy* (New York: Harper and Brothers, 1900), pp. 248–49.

19. Lawrence H. Fuchs, *The American Kaleidoscope: Race, Ethnicity and the Civic Culture* (Middletown, CT: Wesleyan University Press, 1990), p. 283.

20. Emerson, quoted in Rudolph, *American College and University*, p. 241.

21. According to Donald Tewksbury, *The Founding of American Colleges Before the Civil War* (1932) (cited by Hofstadter in his 1955 book *Academic Freedom in the Age of the College*, p. 211), more than five hundred colleges had been established before the Civil War, of which only one hundred survived. More recent studies point out that many of these so-called colleges never got beyond the stage of proposals for creating a new institution. See Natalie A. Naylor, "The Antebellum College Movement," *History of Education Quarterly* 13 (Fall 1973): 261–74.

22. George Ticknor, *Remarks on Changes Lately Proposed or Adopted in Harvard University* (Boston, 1825), p. 40.

23. Michael Rosenthal, *Nicholas Miraculous: The Amazing Career of the Redoubtable Dr. Nicholas Murray Butler* (New York: Farrar, Straus, and Giroux, 2006), p. 75.

24. White, *History of the Warfare of Science with Technology* (New York: Appleton, 1896), 2 vols., 1:vii.

25. In his biography of Butler (*Nicholas Miraculous*), Michael Rosenthal points out (p. 346) that in several "first-rank urban universities" during

the first quarter of the twentieth century, there was serious discussion about consigning undergraduates to "a series of satellite" colleges that would be staffed by separate faculties and likely located out of town.

26. This is Thomas Goodspeed's characterization of Harper's attitude, quoted in Levine, *Powers of the Mind*, p. 40, n. 2.

27. Gerald Graff, *Professing Literature: An Institutional History* (Chicago: University of Chicago Press, 1987), p. 40.

28. Steven Eisman, quoted in Tamar Lewin, "Senator Calls for New Rules for For-Profit Colleges," *New York Times*, June 25, 2010, p. A24. Between 1998 and 2008, enrollment in postsecondary institutions increased overall by just over 30 percent, while enrollment in for-profits increased by 225 percent. And while for-profit institutions account for roughly 10 percent of college enrollment, their students receive almost a quarter of the federal aid for postsecondary students—over $4 billion in 2008–2009, in the form of Pell grants, and nearly $20 billion in federal loans. Tamar Lewin, *New York Times*, July 23, 2010.

29. Alexander C. McCormick and Chun-Mei Zhao, "Rethinking and Reframing the Carnegie Classification," *Change*, September–October 2005.

30. Rudolph, *American College and University*, p. 133.

31. Wertenbaker, *Princeton: 1746–1896*, pp. 304–6; McCosh, in Hofstadter and Smith, *American Higher Education*, 2:720–21.

32. Eliot, in Hofstadter and Smith, *American Higher Education*, 2:705.

33. Eliot, in ibid., 2:711, 706.

34. *Bulletin of Ursinus College*, 2009–10, p. 35.

35. Kerr, *Uses of the University*, p. 49.

36. Eliot, in Hofstadter and Smith, *American Higher Education*, 2:713.

37. Karabel, *The Chosen*, pp. 442–46, describes the administrative maneuvering at Harvard to ensure that admitting female students would result in a minimal reduction in the number of males in the college.

38. Ticknor, *Remarks on Changes in Harvard University*, p. 38.

39. For a recent and representative argument calling for cost savings through large classes on the model of business schools, see Schumpeter, "How to Make College Cheaper," *Economist*, July 9, 2011, p. 64. For the innovation at MIT, see Sara Rimer, "At MIT, Large Lec-

tures Are Going the Way of the Blackboard," *New York Times*, January 13, 2009.

40. Eliot, in Hofstadter and Smith, *American Higher Education*, 2:711.

41. MacIntyre, *Three Rival Versions of Moral Enquiry: Encyclopaedia, Genealogy, and Tradition* (Notre Dame, IN: University of Notre Dame Press, 1990), p. 223. A similar critique has been made by George Marsden, biographer of Jonathan Edwards and a colleague of MacIntyre's at Notre Dame, in *The Soul of the American University: From Protestant Establishment to Established Non-Belief* (New York: Oxford University Press, 1994).

42. Louis Menand, quoted in *Harvard Crimson*, September 4, 2009.

43. In the wake of recent resignations from the Columbia administration, there is some talk of reviving the committee. For an account of the decline of faculty governance in American higher education generally, see Benjamin Ginsberg, *The Fall of the Faculty* (New York: Oxford University Press, 2011).

44. Gilman and Eliot, in Hofstadter and Smith, *American Higher Education*, 2:646, 711.

45. Quoted in Donoghue, *Last Professors*, p. 7.

46. Jonathan Cole, *The Great American Research University* (New York: Public Affairs, 2009), p. 4.

47. Reuben, *Making of the Modern University*, p. 207.

48. McIntyre, *Three Rival Versions*, p. 225.

49. Alvin Kernan, *In Plato's Cave* (New Haven, CT: Yale University Press, 1999), p. 55. Bernadotte Schmidt of the University of Chicago, quoted in Peter Novick, *That Noble Dream: The "Objectivity Question" and the American Historical Profession* (Cambridge: Cambridge University Press, 1988), pp. 223–24.

50. Marc Perry, "The Humanities Go Google," *Chronicle of Higher Education*, May 28, 2010. The quoted comment "literature scholars . . . mapping them instead" is Emily Eakin's paraphrase of the Stanford scholar Franco Moretti, in Eakin, "Studying Literature by the Numbers," *New York Times*, January 10, 2004.

51. According to the "Humanities Indicators" (HI) project (www .humanitiesindicators.org) of the American Academy of Arts and Sci-

ences, students graduating from college in 2009 with a major in the humanities represented approximately 12 percent of all BAs, a fraction that has remained steady over the past twenty years. This figure is based on data available through the Integrated Postsecondary Education Data System (IPEDS) of the Department of Education (http://webcaspar .nsf.gov). Drawing on the same data, the National Science Foundation, however, estimates the percentage of 2009 BAs in the humanities at about 8 percent, also roughly steady since 1989. The discrepancy reflects different assumptions about which fields constitute the humanities. HI includes, for example, theatrical and musical performance and newer fields such as women's, ethnic, and film studies, while NSF does not. By the NSF count, the number of humanities degrees rose over the same period from 82,000 to 123,000, while the more comprehensive HI estimate shows a rise from 114,000 to 186,000. Over the same period, the number of all bachelor's degrees in the United States went from approximately 1 million in 1990 to 1.6 million in 2009. Meanwhile, at elite institutions, both the numbers and percentage of humanities majors have been declining. At Stanford, for instance, the number of humanities majors dropped between 1990 and 2009 from 345 to 256, while the percentage fell from 20.38 percent to 15.4 percent. At Brown, the corresponding numbers are 521 to 340, and 36.5 percent to 23.56 percent; at Yale they are 656 to 429, and 49.58 percent to 32.77 percent. Peer institutions show similar trends, with the notable exception of the University of Chicago, where the number of humanities majors has risen and the percentage dropped only slightly—a combination due to significant expansion of the size of the student body. These data may somewhat overstate the decline of the humanities not only by excluding students who devote themselves to artistic practice or performance and newer academic disciplines, but also because they do not include students completing a second major (roughly 5 percent of all degree earners), some of which may be in a humanistic field. Nor do the data track enrollments by nonmajors in humanities courses, whether required or elective. Despite these caveats, the downward trend seems clear. (Data courtesy of Russell Berman, Stanford University, and David Laurence, MLA Office of Research.)

52. Mara Hvistendahl, "Less Politics, More Poetry: China's Colleges Eye the Liberal Arts," *Chronicle of Higher Education*, January 3, 2010. David Glenn, "Business Curricula Need a Strong Dose of the Liberal Arts, Scholars Say," *Chronicle of Higher Education*, January 21, 2011. For an interesting attempt in the 1950s to design a course of study for business executives, see Morse Peckham, *Humanistic Education for Business Executives: An Essay in General Education* (Philadelphia: University of Pennsylvania Press, 1960). In medical schools, the growing field of medical humanities engages doctors-in-training in discussing works of literature and art as part of a curriculum designed to deepen their sensitivity to their patients. For a directory of programs, see http://medhum.med.nyu.edu/directory.html.

53. Rachel Hadas, *Strange Relation: A Memoir of Marriage, Dementia, and Poetry* (Philadelphia: Paul Dry Books, 2011), p. 41.

Chapter Four. Who Went? Who Goes? Who Pays?

1. Weber, "The Chinese Literati" (1915), in Gerth and Mills, ed., *From Max Weber*, p. 426. Weber's analysis was anticipated in some respects by Immanuel Kant, *The Conflict of the Faculties* (1798).

2. John McNees, "The Quest at Princeton for the Cocktail Soul," *Harvard Crimson*, February 21, 1958.

3. W. Barksdale Maynard, *Woodrow Wilson: Princeton to the Presidency* (New Haven, CT: Yale University Press, 2008), p. 96.

4. Johnson, *Stover at Yale*, p. 265.

5. Today there is a vestige of the practice of conditional acceptance in cases where Ivy League colleges admit certain students on the condition that they take a "gap year" before matriculating.

6. Karabel, *The Chosen*, p. 199.

7. Eliot, quoted in Karabel, *The Chosen*, p. 41.

8. See Rosenthal, *Nicholas Miraculous*, pp. 332–52, and Diana Trilling, *The Beginning of the Journey* (New York: Harcourt, Brace, 1993), p. 269.

9. Lowell, quoted in Karabel, *The Chosen*, p. 51.

10. George Anthony Weller, *Not to Eat, Not for Love* (New York: Harrison Smith and Robert Haas, 1933), pp. 16–17, 37.

11. Theodore H. White, *In Search of History: A Personal Adventure* (New York: Harper Collins, 1978), pp. 42–43.

12. Karabel, *The Chosen*, pp. 259, 213; Archibald Cox et al., *Crisis at Columbia: Report of the Fact-Finding Commission Appointed to Investigate the Disturbances at Columbia University in April and May, 1968* (New York: Vintage Books, 1968), p. 16.

13. See Claudia Goldin and Lawrence Katz, *The Race Between Education and Technology* (Cambridge: Harvard University Press, 2008).

14. A view attributed to Diderot in Richard Sennett, *The Craftsman* (New Haven, CT: Yale University Press, 2008), p. 281.

15. Simeon Baldwin to James Kent, quoted in Robert Middlekauff, *Ancients and Axioms: Secondary Education in 18th Century New England* (New Haven, CT: Yale University Press, 1963), p. 119.

16. Eliot, in Hofstadter and Smith, *American Higher Education*, 2:613; Rudolph, *American College and University*, p. 418.

17. William James, "The Social Value of the College Bred," *McClure's Magazine* 30 (1908). Harold Hyman, *American Singularity: The 1787 Northwest Ordinance, the 1862 Homestead and Morrill Acts, and the 1944 G.I. Bill* (Athens: University of Georgia Press, 1986), p. 70.

18. Karabel, *The Chosen*, p. 183.

19. The development of need-based aid was led by John U. Monro, a Harvard dean who eventually left to teach black students at Miles College in Alabama and later at Tougaloo College in Mississippi. For a clear statement of the original principles of need-based aid, see Monro, "Helping the Student Help Himself," *College Board Review*, May 1953.

20. Tocqueville, *Democracy in America* (1835–40), trans. Arthur Goldhammer (New York: Library of America, 2004), p. 58.

21. Mitchell L. Stevens, *Creating a Class: College Admissions and the Education of Elites* (Cambridge: Harvard University Press, 2007), p. 93.

22. See Thomas J. Espenshade and Alexandria Walton Radford, *No Longer Separate, Not Yet Equal: Race and Class in Elite College Admission and Campus Life* (Princeton, NJ: Princeton University Press, 2009), esp. pp. 108, 299, who state that "with the information at hand," they "are not able to settle the question of whether Asian applicants experience discrimination in elite college admissions" (p. 95).

23. Heller, quoted in Paul Attewell and David E. Lavin, *Does Higher Education for the Disadvantaged Pay Off across the Generations?* (New York: Russell Sage Foundation, 2007), p. 199; Brian K. Fitzgerald and Jennifer A. Delaney, "Educational Opportunity in America," in *Condition of Access: Higher Education for Lower Income Students*, ed. Donald E. Heller (Westport, CT: American Council on Education/ Praeger, 2002).

24. See Clifford Adelman, *The Toolbox Revisited: Paths to Degree Completion from High School through College* (Washington, DC: U.S. Department of Education, 2006).

25. Peter Sacks, *Tearing Down the Gates: Confronting the Class Divide in American Education* (Berkeley: University of California Press, 2007), p. 167.

26. Ibid., p. 169.

27. Between 2008–2009 and 2009–2010, need-based aid grew faster (by 4.6 percent) than merit-based aid (1.2 percent)—but it is too soon to tell if this marks a reversal of the long-term trend. "Mixed News on State Aid," *InsideHigherEd.com*, July 11, 2011.

28. Sacks, *Tearing Down the Gates*, p. 178.

29. This is true as well at public institutions. For California residents, for example, qualifying for state-subsidized tuition at UCLA or Berkeley does not require means testing, so a child of a trust and estate attorney in Marin County may pay roughly the same amount as the child of a municipal worker in Oakland. Since many students at these "flagship" campuses come from middle- and upper-middle-class families, some economists argue that the system amounts to a regressive public subsidy disproportionately benefiting the relatively affluent. See W. Lee Hansen and Burton A. Weisbrod, "The Distribution of Costs and Direct Benefits of Public Higher Education: The Case of California," *Journal of Human Resources* 4 (Spring 1969): 176–91. A useful discussion of the pros and cons of their argument is Thomas J. Kane, *The Price of Admission: Rethinking how Americans Pay for College* (Washington DC: Brookings Institution Press, 1999), pp. 132–33. For illustrations of comparative subsidies enjoyed by students from different socioeconomic strata, see Kane, *Price of Admission*, Table 2-3, p. 38.

30. Ironically, following the crash of 2008 the strain was especially severe at some well-endowed colleges, which rely more than "tuition-dependent" institutions on investment returns for balancing their budgets. For an illustration of the rising pressures on one institution, Reed College, whose commitment to financial aid was tested by the drop in its endowment between 2008 and 2009 (it fell from roughly $450 million to $330 million), see Jonathan D. Glater, "College in Need Closes a Door to Needy Students," *New York Times*, June 9, 2009.

31. Veblen, *Higher Learning in America*, p. 78.

32. Much of the increase in the number of students applying to selective colleges is due to the wide adoption of the "Common Application," an electronic form that makes it easier for candidates (those who can afford multiple application fees) to apply to many institutions. Moreover, colleges inflate their applicant numbers by direct-marketing techniques to students whose names they obtain by buying lists from standardized-test providers—although they know that many of the applications they solicit are from unqualified candidates. Janet Lorin, "SAT Test Owner to Face Query on Teen Privacy from Lawmakers," Bloomberg Education Group, May 26, 2011, www.bloombergeducationgroup@bloomberg.com; Kevin Carey, "Real College-Acceptance Rates Are Higher Than You Think," *Chronicle of Higher Education*, April 19, 2010; Eric Hoover, "College Applications Continue to Increase: When Is Enough Enough?" *New York Times*, November 7, 2010; and Jerome A. Lucido, "Breaking the 'Cruel Cycle of Selectivity' in Admissions," *Chronicle of Higher Education*, January 16, 2011. A valuable report on the state of selective college admissions is *The Case for Change in College Admissions: A Call for Individual and Collective Leadership*, issued in September 2011, by the University of Southern California Center for Enrollment Research, Policy, and Practice in partnership with the Education Conservancy.

33. Sternberg, *College Admissions for the 21st Century* (Cambridge: Harvard University Press, 2010), p. x. Michaels, *The Trouble with Diversity: How We Learned to Love Identity and Ignore Inequality* (New York: Metropolitan Books, 2006), p. 98.

34. The ad was in *Harvard Magazine*, July–August, 2011, p. 79. See www .applicationbootcamp.com and www.ivywise.com, and Jacques Steinberg, "Before College, Costly Advice Just on Getting In," *New York Times*, July 18, 2009. Michaels, *Trouble with Diversity*, p. 87.

35. For thoughtful reviews of some of the ethical issues that arise in college admissions, see two articles by Michael McPherson and Morton Schapiro, "The Search for Morality in Financial Aid," *Academe* (November–December 1993): 23–25; and "Moral Reasoning and Higher-Education Policy," *Chronicle of Higher Education*, September 7, 2007.

36. Kronman, "Is Diversity a Value in American Higher Education?" *Florida Law Review*, December 2000, p. 40. At Yale, in the early 1950s, nearly three-quarters of alumni sons who applied were accepted (see Richard Kahlenberg, ed., *Affirmative Action for the Rich: Legacy Preferences in College Admissions* (New York: Century Foundation, 2010, p. 137). By the 1960s, that figure was still more than two-thirds (Bowen et al., *Equity and Excellence*, p. 169). Today, according to Yale dean of admissions Jeffrey Brenzel, around one in five legacy candidates are admitted, still more than twice the rate for other applicants (Jenny Anderson, "Debating Legacy Admissions at Yale, and Elsewhere," *New York Times*, April 29, 2011). Depending on one's point of view, this is a glass-half-empty or glass-half-full situation. For arguments against legacy admissions, see Kahlenberg, ed., *Affirmative Action for the Rich*. For a defense of legacy admissions as a form of "tolerable corruption," see Russell K. Nieli, "A Reluctant Vote for Legacies," Minding the Campus, February 14, 2011, www.mindingthecampus.com.

37. Roger Lehecka and Andrew Delbanco, "Ivy-League Let Down," *New York Times*, January 23, 2008; Theda Skocpol and Suzanne Mettler, "Back to School," *Democracy: A Journal of Ideas* (Fall 2008): 8–18. See also Richard Ekman, "Free Ride to College? Bearing the Brunt of Changing Expectations on Who Should Pay for College," *University Business*, April 2008. Ekman calls the new policy "affirmative action for the upper middle class."

38. Eric Hoover, "The Flock of Early Birds Keeps Growing," *Chronicle of Higher Education*, November 18, 2011. The best study of the effects of early admissions programs is Christopher Avery, Andrew Fairbanks, and Richard Zeckhauser, *The Early Admissions Game: Joining the Elite* (Cambridge: Harvard University Press, 2003). See also Bowen et al., *Equity and Excellence*, pp. 173–75; and, for a thoughtful response to the resumption of early admissions at Harvard, Geoffrey W. Challen, "Early Inaction: College vs. Country," *Harvard Crimson*, March 2, 2011.

39. The figures are from Bowen et al., *Equity and Excellence*. The eleven institutions are Barnard, Columbia, Oberlin, Penn State, Princeton, Smith, Swarthmore, the University of Pennsylvania, Wellesley, Williams, and Yale. When the sample is broadened to include the "top 146 colleges," as reported in the *Chronicle of Higher Education* (Karin Fischer, "Elite Colleges Lag in Serving the Needy," May 12, 2006), the figure falls to 3 percent. Bowen also reports that only 3 percent of students at nineteen selective colleges and leading state universities are both low-income and first-generation college goers (p. 163).

40. Bowen et al., *Equity and Excellence*, p. 162.

41. "Despite Surging Endowments, High-Ranking Universities and Colleges Show Disappointing Results in Enrolling Low-Income Students," *Journal of Blacks in Higher Education*, January 6, 2008. David Leonhart, "Top Colleges, Largely for the Elite," *New York Times*, May 24, 2011.

42. Michaels, *Trouble with Diversity*, p. 17.

43. See *Trends in College Spending: Where Does the Money Come From? Where Does It Go?* Delta Cost Project and Lumina Foundation for Education, 2008, available at www.deltacostproject.org; and David Levinson, "Grand Solution or Grab Bag," *American Prospect*, November, 2009, p. A15.

44. See Arum and Jopska, *Academically Adrift*; and William G. Bowen, Matthew M. Chingos, and Michael S. McPherson, *Crossing the Finish Line: Completing College at America's Public Universities* (Princeton, NJ: Princeton University Press, 2009).

45. Peter Orszag, "A Health Care Plan for Colleges," *New York Times*, September 18, 2010, argues that the rising cost of Medicaid accounts

in large measure for declining support of public higher education in the budgeting priorities of the states. Orszag, former director of the White House Office of Management and Budget under President Obama, points out that over the last thirty years, faculty salaries at public universities have gone from rough parity with their private counterparts to a shortfall of at least 20 percent.

Chapter Five. Brave New World

1. Karabel, *The Chosen*, p. 5.
2. John Murray Cuddihy, *The Ordeal of Civility: Freud, Marx, Lévi-Strauss, and the Jewish Struggle with Modernity* (New York: Basic Books, 1974), p. 5; Owen Johnson, *Stover at Yale*, p. 176.
3. Eliot, in Hofstadter and Smith, *American Higher Education*, 2:614.
4. See Richard F. Miller, *Harvard's Civil War: A History of the Twentieth Massachusetts Volunteer Infantry* (Lebanon, NH: University Press of New England, 2005). Shaw and his troops are the subject of a bronze memorial frieze by Augustus Saint Gaudens overlooking the Boston Common.
5. James, *The Bostonians* (1886; Baltimore: Penguin, 1966), p. 210.
6. Johnson, *Stover at Yale*, p. 186.
7. Ibid., pp. 29, 68.
8. Geoffrey Kabaservice, *The Guardians: Kingman Brewster, His Circle, and the Rise of the Liberal Establishment* (New York: Henry Holt, 2004).
9. Auchincloss, *The Rector of Justin* (Boston: Houghton-Mifflin, 1964), p. 33.
10. Ibid., pp. 45, 39.
11. Karabel, *The Chosen*, p. 35.
12. Young, *The Rise of the Meritocracy, 1870–2033* (London: Penguin Books, 1961), p. 92.
13. Ibid, p. 116.
14. Ibid, pp. 106–7.
15. Ibid., pp. 167–68.
16. Ibid, p. 74. Even in our brave new world of "attention deficit disorder" and Ritalin, students who are strong in one academic area and

weak in another (as reflected in "berserk" records of As in some subjects and Bs or Cs in others) are much less likely to gain admission to top colleges than they would have been a generation ago.

17. Michaels, *Trouble with Diversity*, pp. 97, 104. Michaels argues that race-conscious admissions functions for white students in elite colleges as "a powerful tool for legitimizing their sense of their individual merit" by fostering the notion that minority students are the beneficiaries of exceptional allowances.

18. See Shamus Khan, "Meritocracy Is an Engine of Inequality," *Columbia Spectator*, March 3, 2011, which describes a system in which "the winners think they've won because of their merit, not their advantages."

19. Quoted in Ben Wildavsky, *The Great Brain Race: How Global Universities Are Shaping the World* (Princeton, NJ: Princeton University Press, 2010), p. 125.

20. Ibid., p. 171.

21. Jack Matthews, "Nathaniel Hawthorne's Untold Tale," *Chronicle of Higher Education*, August 15, 2010.

22. Miller, *Harvard's Civil War*, p. 3; Melville, "The College Colonel," in *Battle-Pieces and Aspects of the War* (1866).

23. Michaels, *Trouble with Diversity*, p. 85. Ross Gregory Douthat, *Privilege: Harvard and the Education of the Ruling Class* (New York: Hyperion, 2005), pp. 12–13.

24. John Cotton, *A Treatise of the Covenant of Grace*, in *The Puritans in America*, ed. Alan Heimert and Andrew Delbanco (Cambridge: Harvard University Press, 1985), p.151.

25. Karabel, *The Chosen*, p. 557.

26. Kirn, *The Daily Beast*, May 19, 2009. These are essentially the same characters whom David Brooks, a graduate of the University of Chicago, described as "Bobos" (a hybrid of "bourgeois" and "bohemian") in his best-selling book *Bobos in Paradise: The New Upper Class and How They Got There* (New York: Simon and Schuster, 2000). Two biting articles about the sense of entitlement among students at Harvard and Yale are John Summers, "All the Privileged Must Have Prizes," *Times Higher Education Supplement* (London), July 19, 2008;

and William Deresiewicz, "The Disadvantages of an Elite Education," *American Scholar* 77, no. 3 (Summer 2008): 20–31.

27. William Bowen, *Lessons Learned: Reflections of a University President*
(Princeton, NJ: Princeton University Press, 2011), pp. 33–34. Between 2001 and 2008–2009, the number of public-university presidents earning more than half a million dollars rose nearly tenfold,
from six to fifty-eight. For an account of the "cozy and lucrative club"
of academic leaders, see Graham Bowley, "The Academic-Industrial
Complex," *New York Times*, July 31, 2010. It should be noted that
the Illinois chancellor donates her board salary to support student
scholarships. See Erik Siemers, "Nike Director named U. of Illinois
Chancellor," *Portland Business Journal*, August 5, 2011.

28. Henry Rosovsky, "Annual Report of the Dean of the Faculty of
Arts and Sciences, 1990–1991," *Policy Perspectives* 4, no. 3 (Septem-
ber 1992): 1b–2b. Sewell Chan, "Academic Economists to Consider
Ethics Code," *New York Times*, December 31, 2010. On the Qaddafi
matter, see David Corn, "Monitor Group: Still Spinning?" *Mother
Jones*, March 3, 2011; and Paul A. Rahe, "The Intellectual as Courtier,"
Chronicle of Higher Education, March 7, 2011.

29. John Jay Chapman, "The Function of a University" (1900), in *Un-
bought Spirit: A John Jay Chapman Reader*, ed. Richard Stone (Ur-
bana: University of Illinois Press, 1998), p. 93; James Engell and
Anthony Dangerfield, *Saving Higher Education in the Age of Money*
(Charlottesville: University of Virginia Press, 2005); David Kirp,
*Shakespeare, Einstein, and the Bottom Line: The Marketing of Higher
Education* (Cambridge: Harvard University Press, 2003); Jenni-
fer Washburn, *University, Inc.: The Corporate Corruption of Higher
Education* (New York: Basic Books, 2005); Carlos Alonso, "Paradise
Lost: The Academy Becomes a Commodity," *Chronicle of Higher
Education*, December 12, 2010.

30. Joseph O'Neill, *Netherland* (New York: Pantheon, 2008), p. 91.

31. Robert Pollack, "I Am, Therefore I Think," *Columbia Spectator*,
September 16, 2010. In his autobiography *The Bridge*, Ernest Poole
(Princeton, class of 1902) writes that during his college days, only once
did he see a cheating incident. Sitting behind the cheater during an

exam was the class president, who, seeing his classmate "furtively . . . looking at notes," whispered in his ear, "Tear up your paper and flunk this" (quoted in Wertenbaker, *Princeton, 1746–1896*, p. 364). Suitably shamed, the culprit obliged. This kind of peer-group policing seems less prevalent today. One question, about which frank discussion is hard to come by, is whether cultural differences regarding issues such as originality and imitation are part of the problem as Asian students (both foreign-born and the children of immigrants) enter U.S. colleges in large numbers. See Elizabeth Redden, "Cheating Across Cultures," *InsideHigherEd.com*, May 24, 2007; and Kelly Heyboer, "Centenary College Closes Satellite Schools in China, Taiwan after Finding Rampant Cheating," *NJ.com*, July 25, 2010, www.NJ.com.

32. William Dowling, *Spoilsport: My Life and Hard Times Fighting Sports Corruption at an Old Eastern University* (University Park: Penn State University Press, 2007); Murray Sperber, *Beer and Circus: How Big-Time College Sports Is Crippling Undergraduate Education* (New York: Henry Holt, 2000). Quoted in Philip Kay, "'Guttersnipes' and 'Eliterates': City College in the Popular Imagination" (PhD diss., Columbia University, 2011), p. 264.

33. Erick Smith, "Stanford Discontinuing 'Easy' Class List for Athletes," *USA Today*, March 9, 2011; "The Early Admissions Loophole," *InsideHigherEd.com*, October 19, 2006. James L. Shulman and William G. Bowen, *The Game of Life: College Sports and Educational Values* (Princeton, NJ: Princeton University Press, 2001.) In a highly critical discussion of college athletics as a drain on institutional resources, Derek Bok, *Universities in the Marketplace: The Commercialization of Higher Education* (Princeton, NJ: Princeton University Press, 2003), chap. 3, points out that "the cost of intercollegiate athletics dwarfs the amounts made available for community service, student orchestras, theater, and other worthwhile extracurricular activities" (p. 41). For the practice of sending out "likely letters" during the (temporary) suspension of early admissions, see Lingbo Li, "Likely Letters on the Rise," *Harvard Crimson*, March 13, 2008.

34. Andrew Dickson White, president of Cornell (1873), quoted in Bok, *Universities in the Marketplace*, p. 55; Bowen et al., *Equity and Excellence*, p. 171; Lewis, *Excellence without a Soul*, p. 252.

35. Christopher Jencks and David Riesman, *The Academic Revolution* (1968; New Brunswick, NJ: Transaction, 2002), p. 243.

36. Bok, *Universities in the Marketplace*, p. 30.

Chapter Six. What Is to Be Done?

1. Zephyr Teachout, *Washington Post*, September 13, 2009. See also Sarah Lacy, "Peter Thiel: We're in a Bubble and It's Not the Internet. It's Higher Education," *TechCrunch*, April 10, 2011, www.techcrunch .com. (Thiel is cofounder of PayPal.)

2. Michael S. McPherson and Morton O. Schapiro, "The Future Economic Challenges for the Liberal Arts Colleges," in Koblik and Graubard, eds., *Distinctively American*, pp. 49–50.

3. *New York Times*, August 25, 2010.

4. Clark Kerr, "The American Mixture of Higher Education in Perspective: Four Dimensions," *Higher Education* 19 (1990): 1; American Council on Education, *Fact Book on Higher Education, 1986–1987* (New York: Macmillan, 1987), p. 57; U.S. Department of Education, National Center for Education Statistics, *120 Years of American Education: A Statistical Portrait* (Washington DC: U.S. Department of Education, 1993), table 24, pp. 76–77.

5. Arthur Levine, "Colleges and the Rebirth of the American Dream," *Chronicle of Higher Education*, July 11, 2010; Bowen, Chingos, and McPherson, *Crossing the Finish Line*, p. 30; Jane Wellman, *New York Times*, February 4, 2010; Sara Goldrick-Rab, "Following Their Every Move: An Investigation of Social-Class Differences in College Pathways," *Sociology of Education* 79, no. 1 (January 2006): 61–79.

6. Eugene Tobin, comments to the board of the Teagle Foundation (March 5, 2010), quoted by permission.

7. David Kirp, *Shakespeare, Einstein, and the Bottom Line: The Marketing of Higher Education* (Cambridge: Harvard University Press, 2005), p. 69.

8. Donoghue, *Last Professors*, p. xiv.

9. Diane Auer Jones, "Assessment Changes Online Teaching from an Art to a Science," *Chronicle of Higher Education*, November 6, 2011.

10. Over the last decade, the dollar amount of loans going to students enrolled in for-profit colleges has expanded by nearly 700 percent, from $4 billion in 2000 to $27 billion in 2010 (National Public Radio, *All Things Considered*, August 17, 2010). Some observers, noting the combination of increasing government scrutiny and growing public skepticism about the value of credentials earned from for-profit institutions, believe that this is a business headed for collapse. See Steve Eisman et al., "Subprime Goes to College," Market Folly, May 27, 2010, http://www.marketfolly.com/2010/05/steve-eisman-frontpoint-partners-ira.html.

11. W. Robert Connor and Cheryl Ching, "Can Learning Be Improved When Budgets Are in the Red?" *Chronicle of Higher Education*, April 25, 2010. For a cautionary tale of how the effort to measure educational "outcomes" has affected universities in Britain, see Stefan Collini, "From Robbins to McKinsey," *London Review of Books*, August 25, 2011. Francis Lieber, in Hofstadter and Smith, *American Higher Education*, 1:299. See chap. 1, n. 3.

12. Ticknor, *Remarks on Changes in Harvard University*, p. 35.

13. McCosh, in Hofstadter and Smith, *American Higher Education*, 2:723.

14. Perhaps the most persuasive critical voice in the debate is that of Diane Ravitch, who once supported NCLB but now calls it a "timetable for the destruction of public education." See Ravitch, "Obama's War on Schools," *Newsweek*, March 20, 2011.

15. Cotton Mather, in Hofstadter and Smith, *American Higher Education*, 1:16. Margery Foster, "*Out of Smalle Beginnings: An Economic History of Harvard College in the Puritan Period* (Cambridge: Harvard University Press, 1962), p. 105.

16. Dave Gershman, "Legislative Study Group Explores Idea of Privatizing the University of Michigan," *Ann Arbor News*, December 18, 2008.

17. For an attempt to measure student learning at seventeen colleges and universities, see the Wabash National Study, 2006–2009, at http://

www.liberalarts.wabash.edu/study-research/. On October 26, 2009, *Newsweek* ran a cover story by Senator Lamar Alexander of Tennessee (a former university president and secretary of education), entitled "Why College Should Take Only Three Years." The same idea had been put forward more than one hundred years earlier by, among others, William James, "The Proposed Shortening of the College Course," *Harvard Monthly* 11 (1891).

18. "Board Responsibility for the Oversight of Educational Quality," a report issued March 17, 2011, by the Association of Governing Boards, www.agb.org. See also José A. Cabranes, "Myth and Reality of University Trusteeship in the Post-Enron Era," *Fordham Law Review* 76, no. 2 (November 2007): 955–79.

19. Christopher Jencks, "The Graduation Gap," *American Prospect*, November 18, 2009.

20. Ronald G. Ehrenberg, "How Governments Can Improve Access to College," *Chronicle of Higher Education*, April 6, 2007; Donald Heller, "A Bold Proposal: Increasing College Access without Spending More Money," *Crosstalk*, Fall 2004.

21. See, for instance, Charles Murray, "Intelligence and College," *National Affairs* (Fall 2009): 95–106, who states with remarkable confidence that "only a small minority of high-school graduates have the intelligence to succeed in college."

22. Eliot, in Hofstadter and Smith, *American Higher Education*, 2:604.

23. An exemplary college-community partnership is the Double Discovery Center, founded at Columbia in the 1960s by students and faculty. Through volunteers who are mainly college students, DDC provides over one thousand local middle and high schoolers with tutoring and mentoring, in order to improve their chances of becoming first in their families to attend college. See http://www.columbia.edu/cu/college/ddc/.

24. See Christopher Avery and Thomas J. Kane, "Student Perceptions of College Opportunities: The Boston COACH Program," in *College Choices: The Economics of Where to Go, When to Go, and How to Pay for It*, ed. Caroline M. Hoxby (Chicago: University of Chicago Press, 2004). For a summary of recommendations to clarify and simplify

the process of applying for financial aid, see Michael S. McPherson and Sandy Baum, "Fulfilling the Commitment: Recommendations for Reforming Federal Student Aid," College Board, 2009, www .collegeboard.com/rethinkingstudentaid.

25. Bowen, Chingos, and McPherson, *Crossing the Finish Line*, pp. 204, 219.

26. *New York Times*, April 26, 2009.

27. Emerson, journal entry, September 14, 1839, in Porte, ed., *Emerson in his Journals*, p. 223.

28. Richard L. Morrill, *Strategic Leadership: Integrating Strategy and Leadership in Colleges and Universities* (Westport, CT: American Council on Education/Praeger, 2007), p. 26.

29. See Open Learning Initiative, http://oli.web.cmu.edu/openlearning/, which offers courses in statistics, biochemistry, economics, and other subjects.

30. One interesting experiment is "University of the People," a global on-line university that, up to now, has charged no tuition and minimal processing and examination fees. www.uopeople.org.

31. Cathy Davidson, *Now You See It: How the Brain Science of Attention Will Transform the Way We Live, Work, and Learn* (New York: Viking, 2011). Davidson's vision reminds me of something I heard twenty-five years ago from a job candidate during an interview for an English department teaching position. When asked what he would teach in a course on American poetry, he replied that he preferred the "inductive syllabus"—by which he meant that rather than assigning readings he would ask students to consult some poetry anthologies in the library, and, after they had leafed through them for a bit, he would have them nominate their favorite poems, put the nominees to a class vote, and the winners would constitute the course reading list.

32. Michael Schudson et al., "General Education in the 21st Century: A Report of the University of California Commission on Undergraduate Education," Center for Studies in Higher Education, April 2007, www.cshe.berkeley.edu.

33. For an account of Mazur's practice, see Derek Bok, *Our Under-achieving Colleges: A Candid Look at How Much Students Learn*

and Why They Should Be Learning More (Princeton, NJ: Princeton University Press, 2006), pp. 132–34. For an innovative method of teaching history, whereby students, having read relevant primary and secondary texts, adopt the roles of historical figures and debate contentious issues from the trial of Socrates or Galileo, to the partition of India or Palestine, see Mark Carnes, "Inciting Speech," *Change* (March–April 2005): 6–11. Carnes calls his teaching method "Reacting to the Past."

34. Kronman calls it the "research ideal" (*Education's End*, chap. 3); Menand writes of the decline of general education in favor of "credentialization and specialization" (*Marketplace of Ideas*, p. 101); Hacker and Dreifus speak of "knowledge that professors create for other professors" and of faculty inflicting their "microspecialties" on defenseless undergraduates (*Higher Education?*, p. 85).

35. Emerson, quoted in Bledstein, *Culture of Professionalism*, p. 265.

36. Carol Geary Schneider, "Transformative Learning—Mine and Theirs," in *Literary Study, Measurement, and the Sublime: Disciplinary Assessment*, ed. Donna Heiland and Laura J. Rosenthal (New York: Teagle Foundation, 2011), p. 28.

37. Ronald G. Ehrenberg, Harriet Zuckerman, Jeffrey A. Groen, and Sharon M. Brucker, *Educating Scholars: Doctoral Education in the Humanities* (Princeton, NJ: Princeton University Press, 2010), p. 260.

38. Edward J. Eckenfels, *Doctors Serving People: Restoring Humanism to Medicine Through Student Community Service* (New Brunswick, NJ: Rutgers University Press, 2008), p. 5.

39. Robert Maynard Hutchins, *The Higher Learning in America* (New Haven, CT: Yale University Press, 1936), p. 115.

40. Quoted in Mark Schwehn, *Exiles from Eden: Religion and the Academic Vocation in America* (New York: Oxford University Press, 1993), p. 70.

41. Roald Hoffmann, "Research Strategy: Teach," *American Scientist* 84 (1996): 20–22. See also David F. Feldon et al., "Graduate Students' Teaching Experiences Improve Their Methodological Research Skills," *Science* 333, no. 6045 (August 19, 2011): 1037–39.

42. I have put forward this suggestion in greater detail in "What Should PhD Mean?" *PMLA* 115 (2000): 1205–9.

43. Donald I. Finkel, *Teaching with Your Mouth Shut* (Portsmouth, NH: Boynton/Cook, 2000).

44. John Cotton, *Christ the Fountaine of Life*, p. 119.

45. Emerson, *The American Scholar* (1837), in *Selections from Ralph Waldo Emerson*, ed. Stephen Whicher (Boston: Houghton-Mifflin, 1957), p. 69.

46. Leon Botstein, "Con Ed," *New Republic*, November, 6, 2009; Debra Satz and Rob Reich, "The Liberal Reach," *Dissent* (Winter 2004): 72–75.

47. These words were spoken by Mark DeFusco, former director of the University of Phoenix, on the PBS *Frontline* report, "College Inc.," broadcast May 4, 2010. I owe the reference to an unpublished paper by Christine Smallwood, "What Makes Education So Special: For-Profit Colleges and American Higher Education," Columbia University, spring 2010.

48. Project Pericles, www.projectpericles.org.

49. Noah Porter, *American Colleges and the American Public* (1870), in Cohen, ed., *Education in the United States*, 3:1475; Peter Pouncey, *Rules for Old Men Waiting* (New York: Random House, 2005), pp. 105–6.

50. Trilling, "The America of John Dos Passos," in *The Moral Obligation to be Intelligent: Selected Essays of Lionel Trilling*, ed. Leon Wieseltier (New York: Farrar, Straus, and Giroux, 2000), pp. 6–7.

INDEX

Index

Index

Index